Real World
Colouring Book
For Advanced Users & Adults

50 Images

**Created From Real Life Photos
For You To Colour As You Please.**

ISBN 978-0-359-86336-5
90000
9 780359 863365

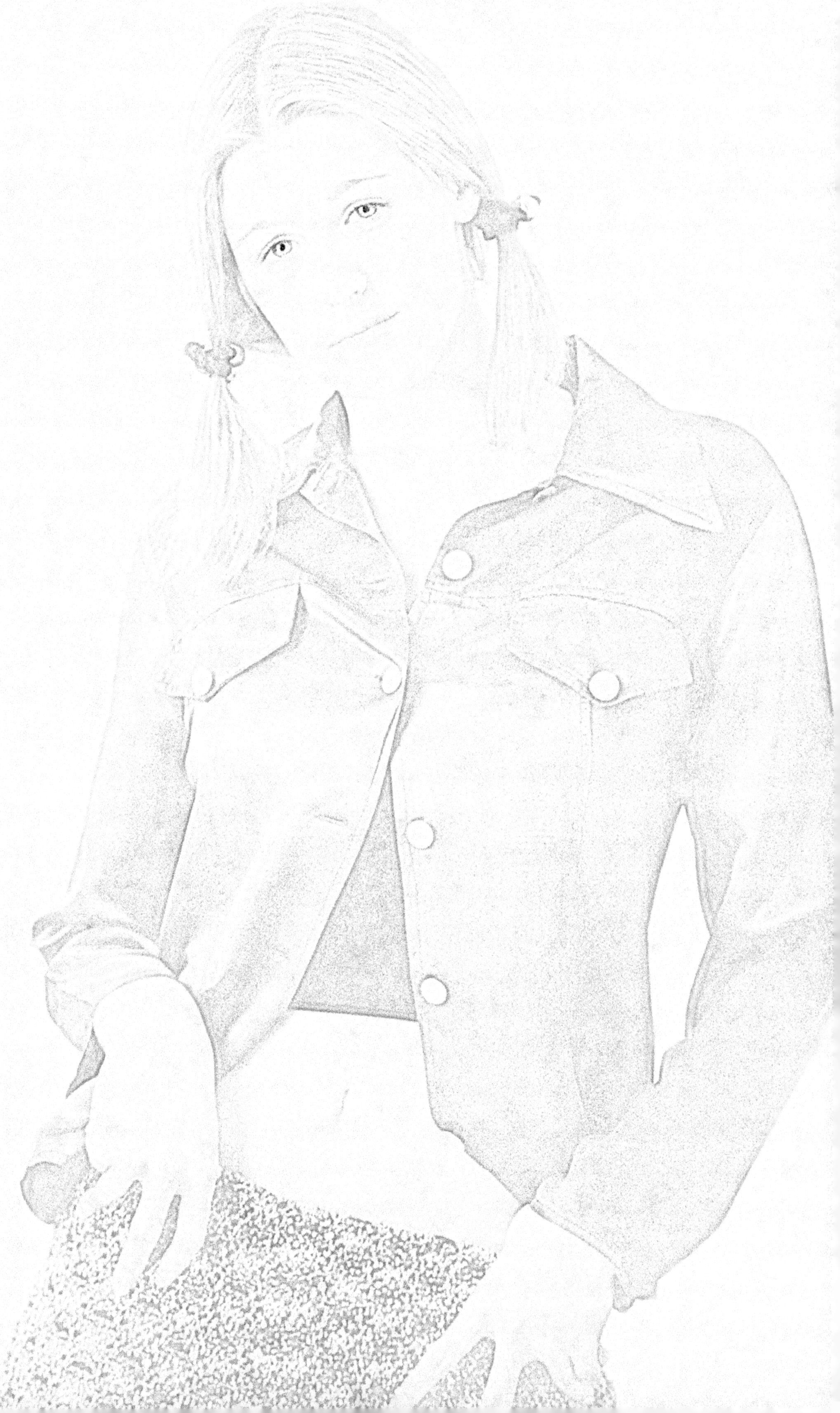

POST

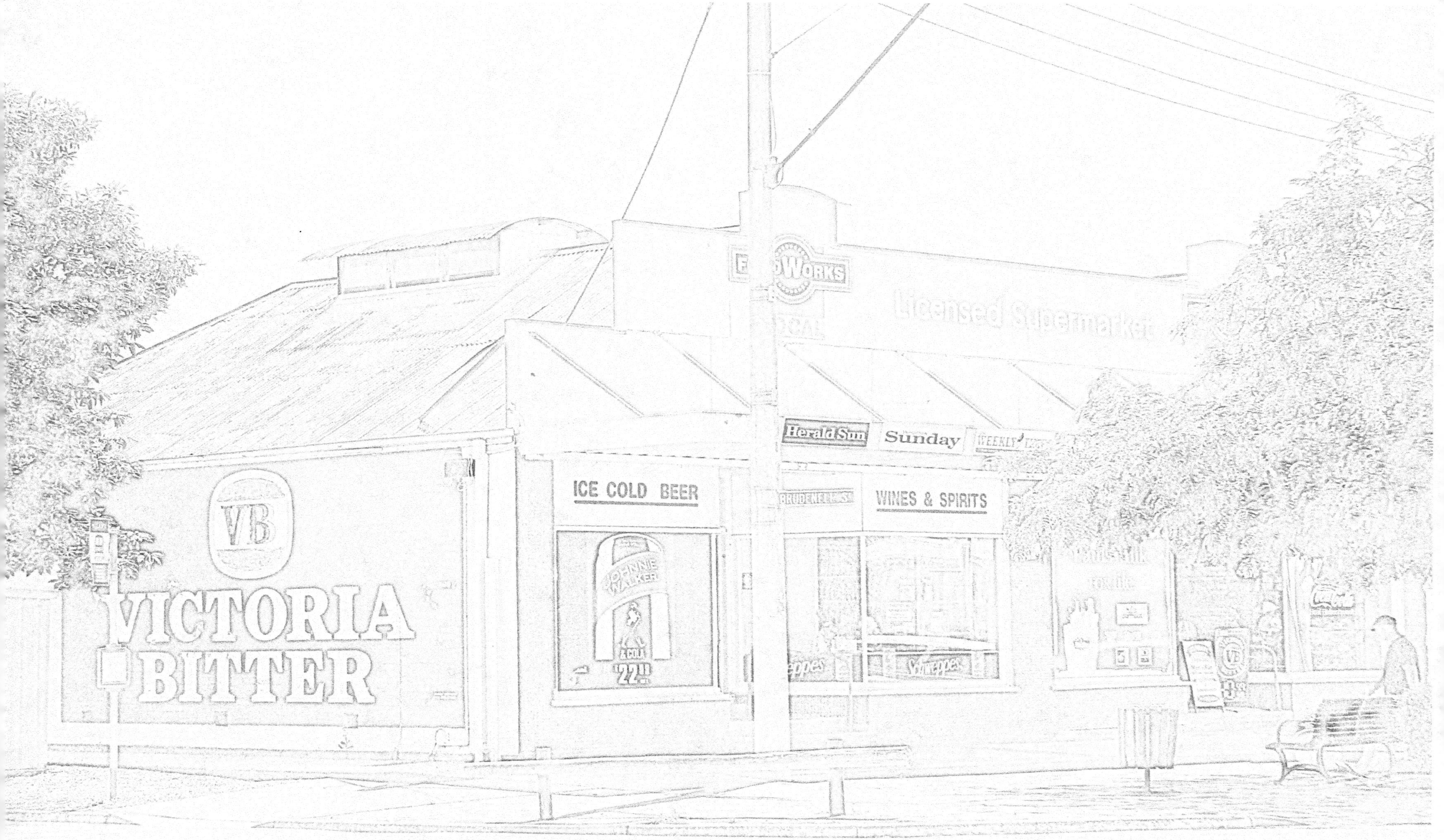
Licensed Supermarket
Herald Sun
Sunday
ICE COLD BEER
WINES & SPIRITS
VB
VICTORIA
BITTER
JOHNNIE WALKER
"22"

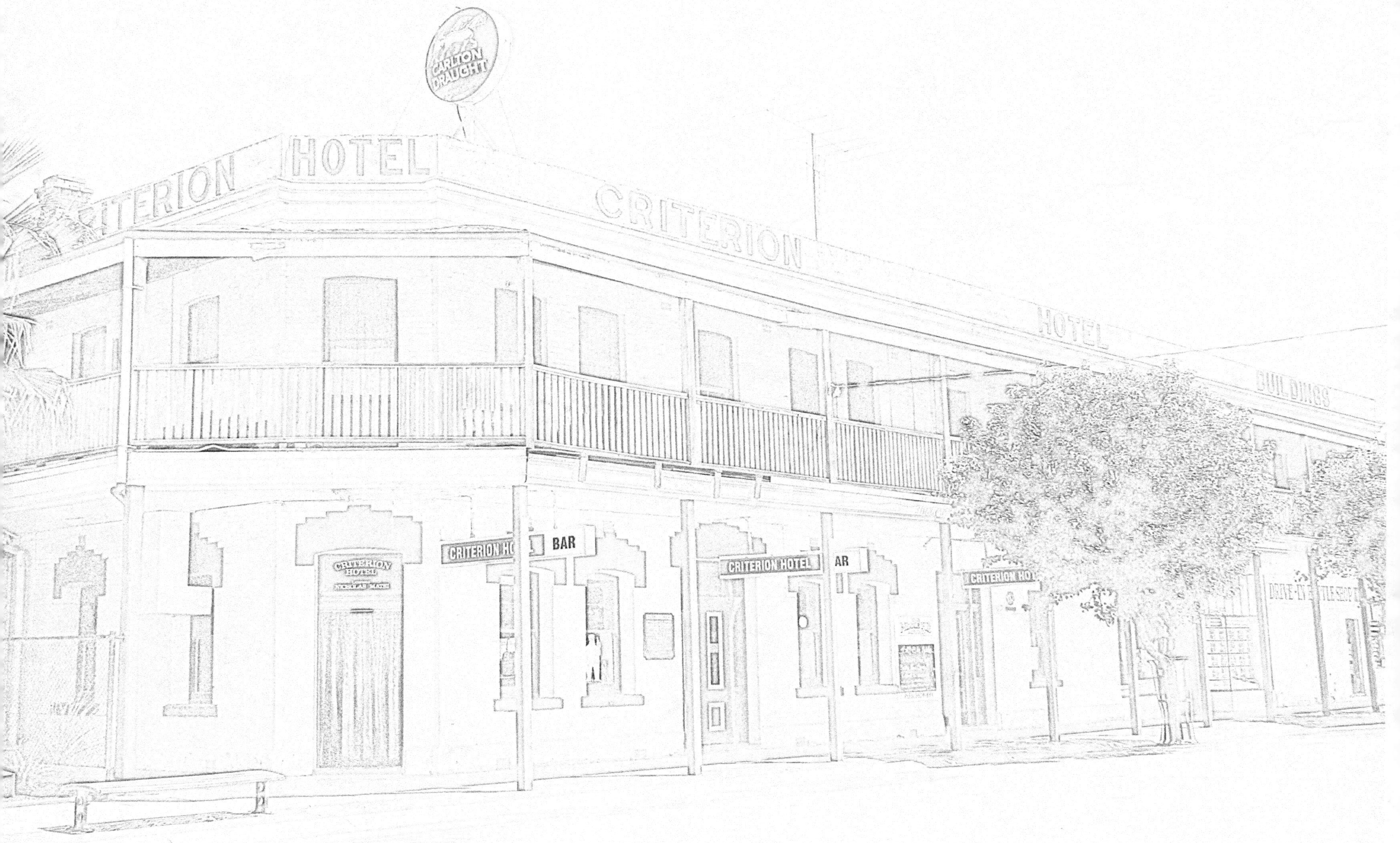
CARLTON DRAUGHT
CRITERION HOTEL
CRITERION HOTEL
BUILDINGS
CRITERION HOTEL
CRITERION HOTEL BAR
CRITERION HOTEL
BAR

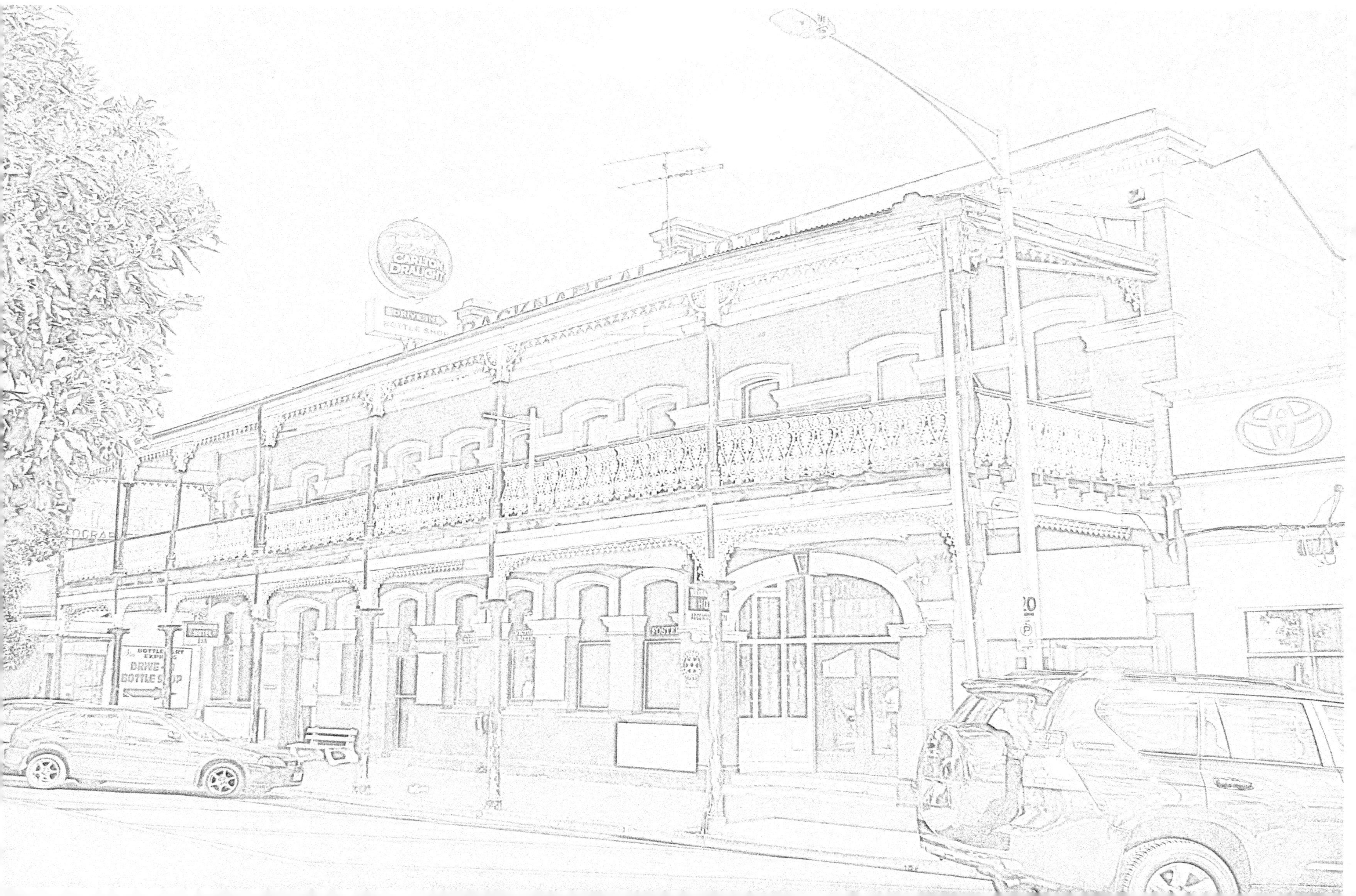
CARLTON DRAUGHT
DRIVE-IN
BOTTLE SHOP
DRIVE-IN
BOTTLE SHOP
FOSTER'S

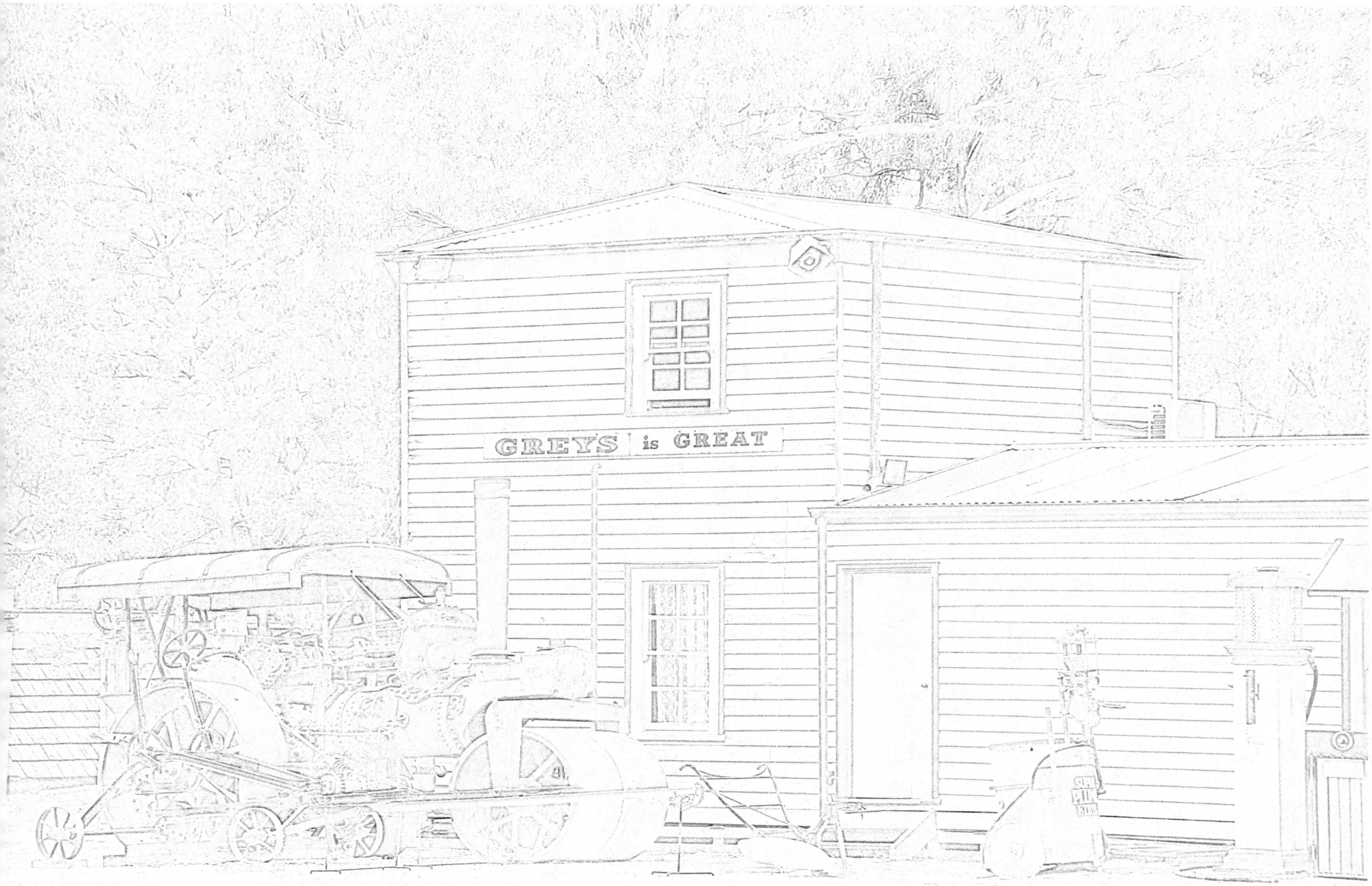
GREYS is GREAT

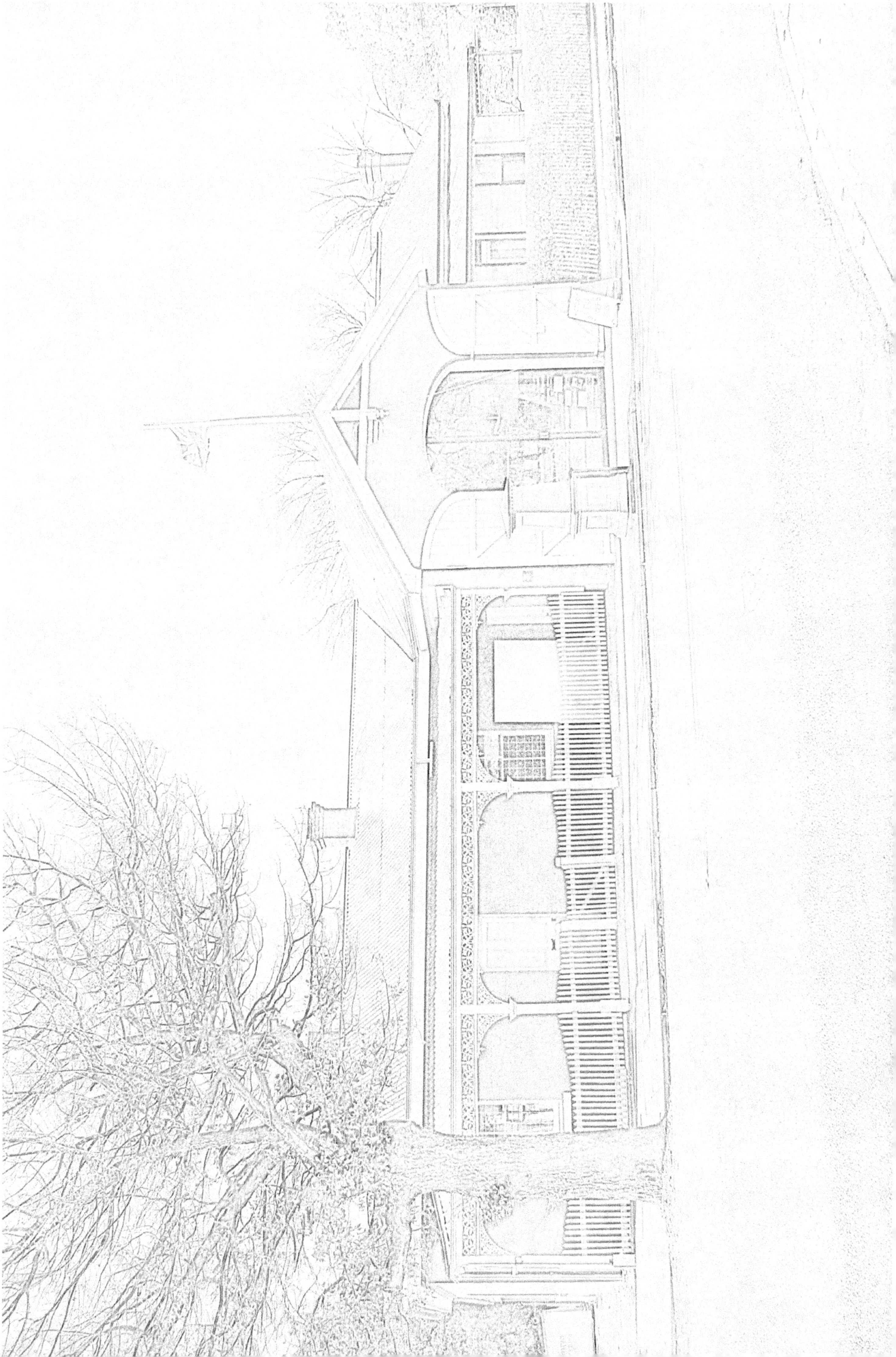

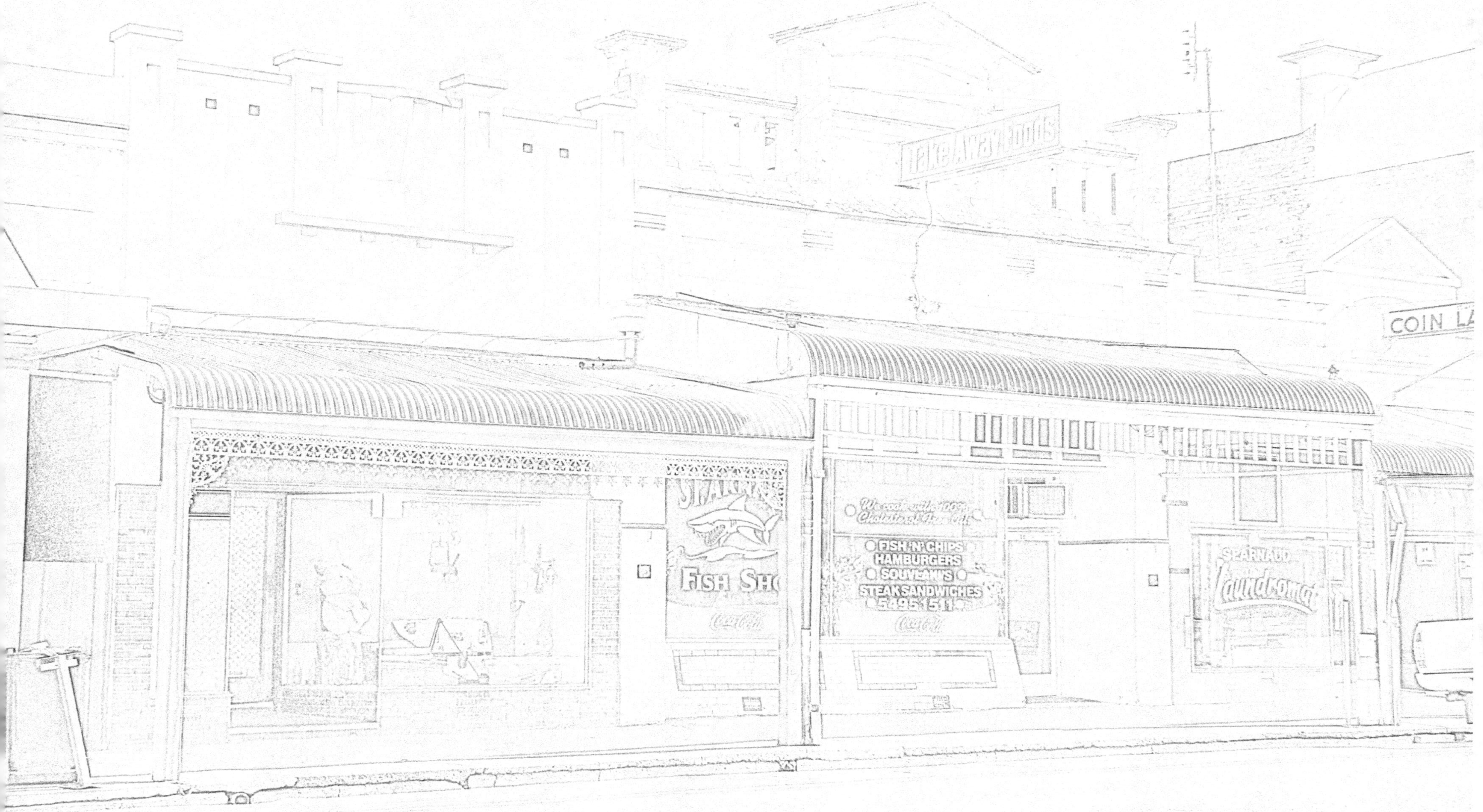
COIN LA
Take Away Foods
Laundromat
FISH 'N' CHIPS
HAMBURGERS
STEAK SANDWICHES
Coca-Cola
FISH SHO
Coca-Cola

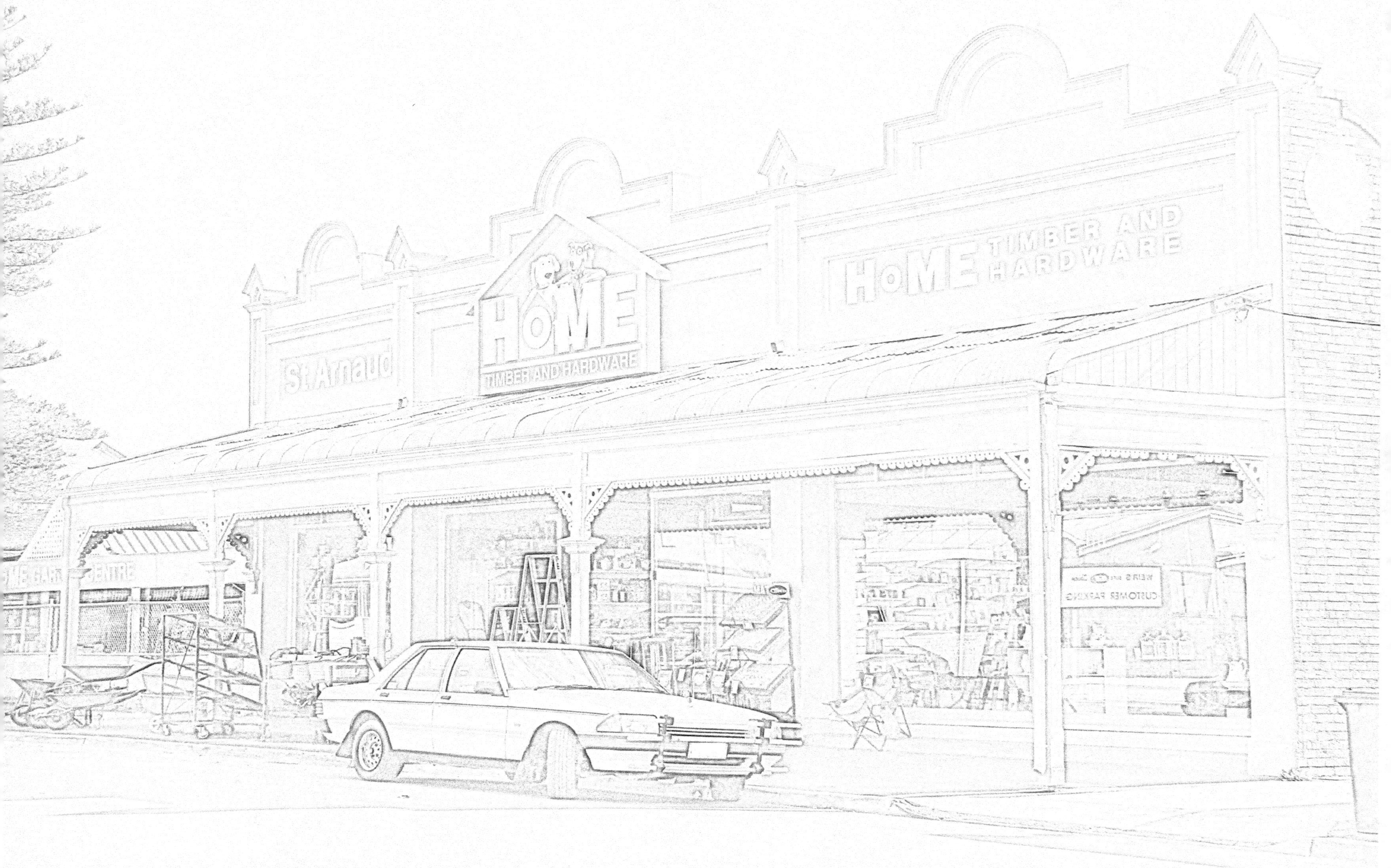
St Arnaud
HOME
TIMBER AND HARDWARE
HOME TIMBER AND HARDWARE
CUSTOMER PARKING

1872
1939
TOWN
HALL

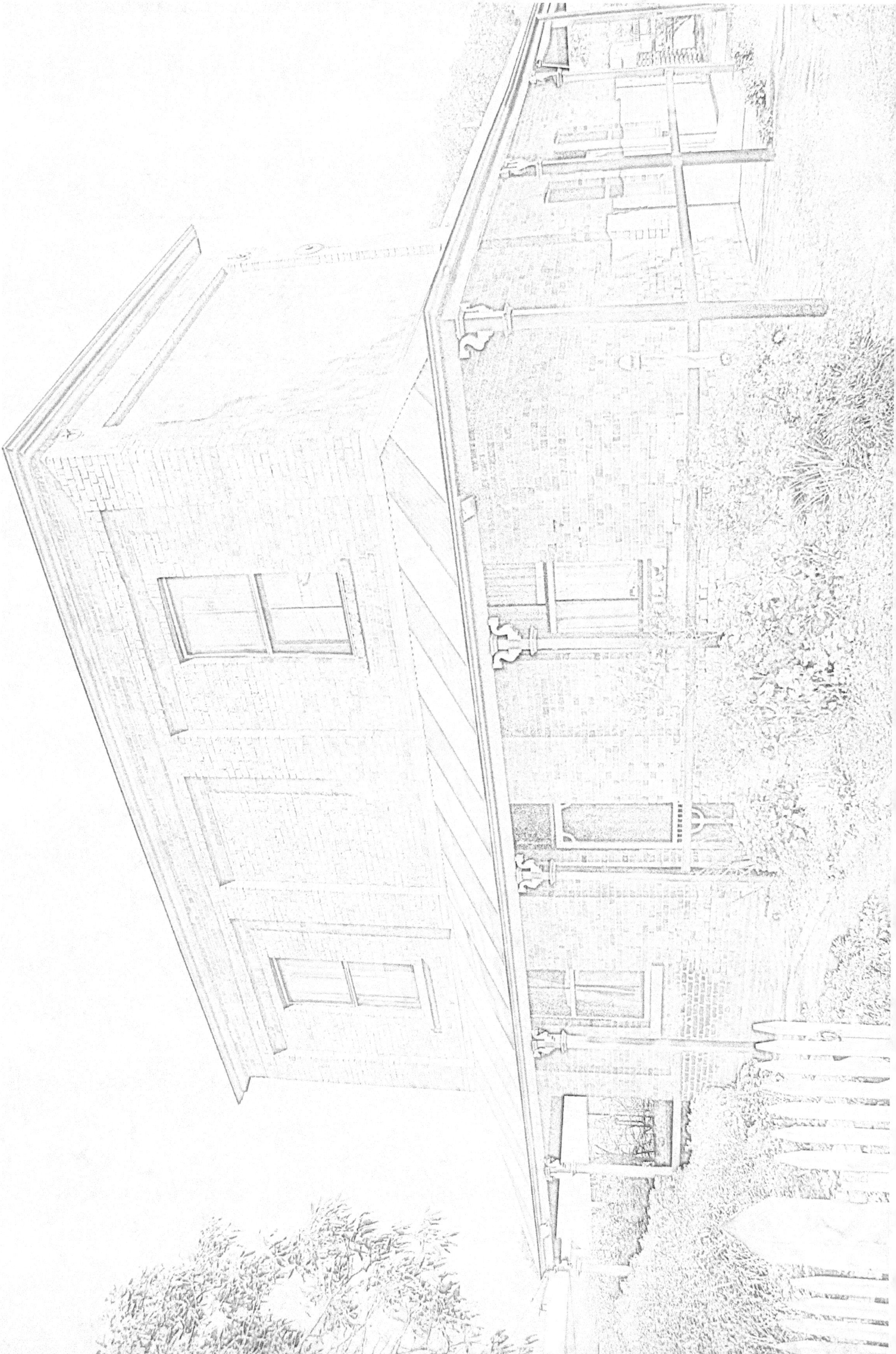

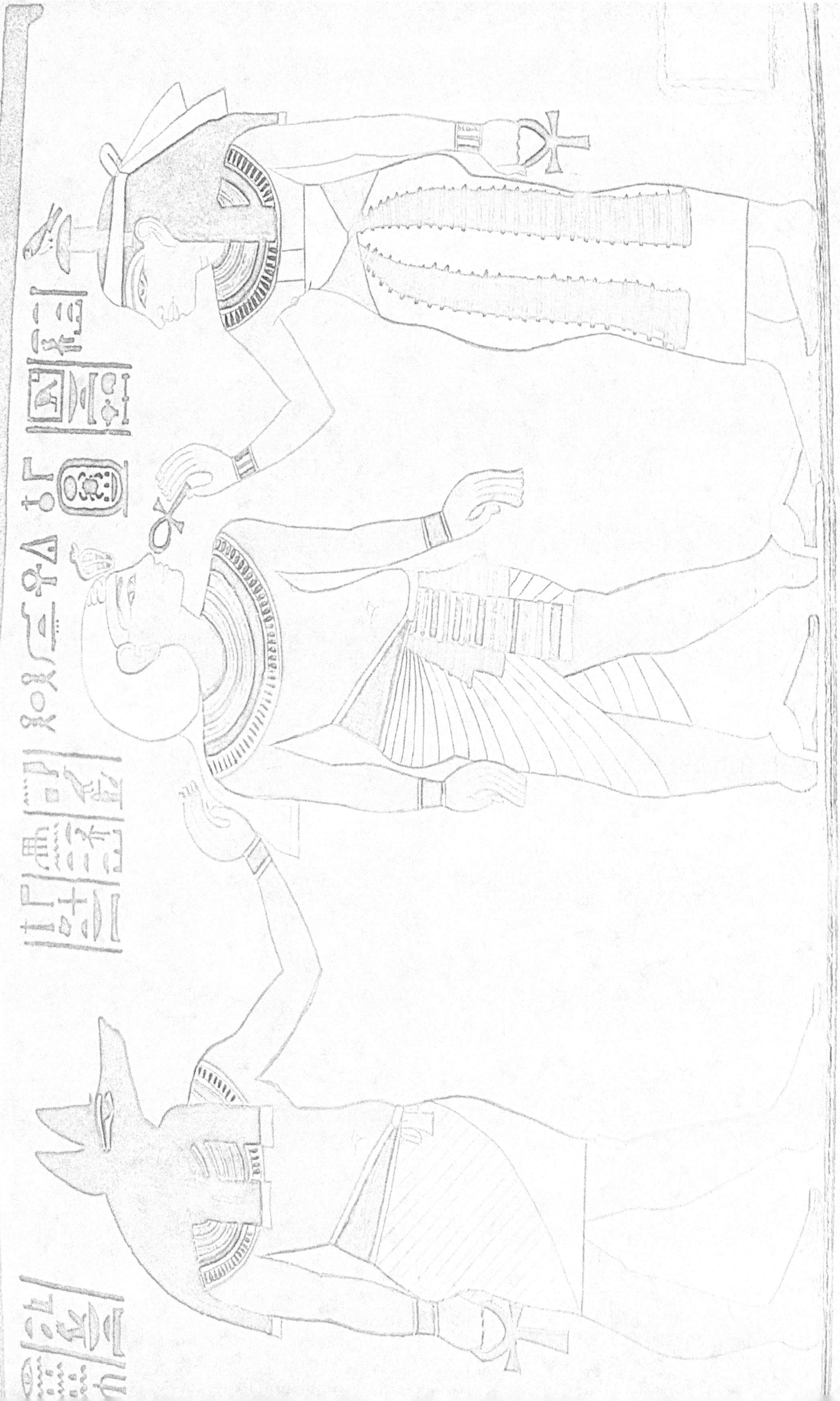

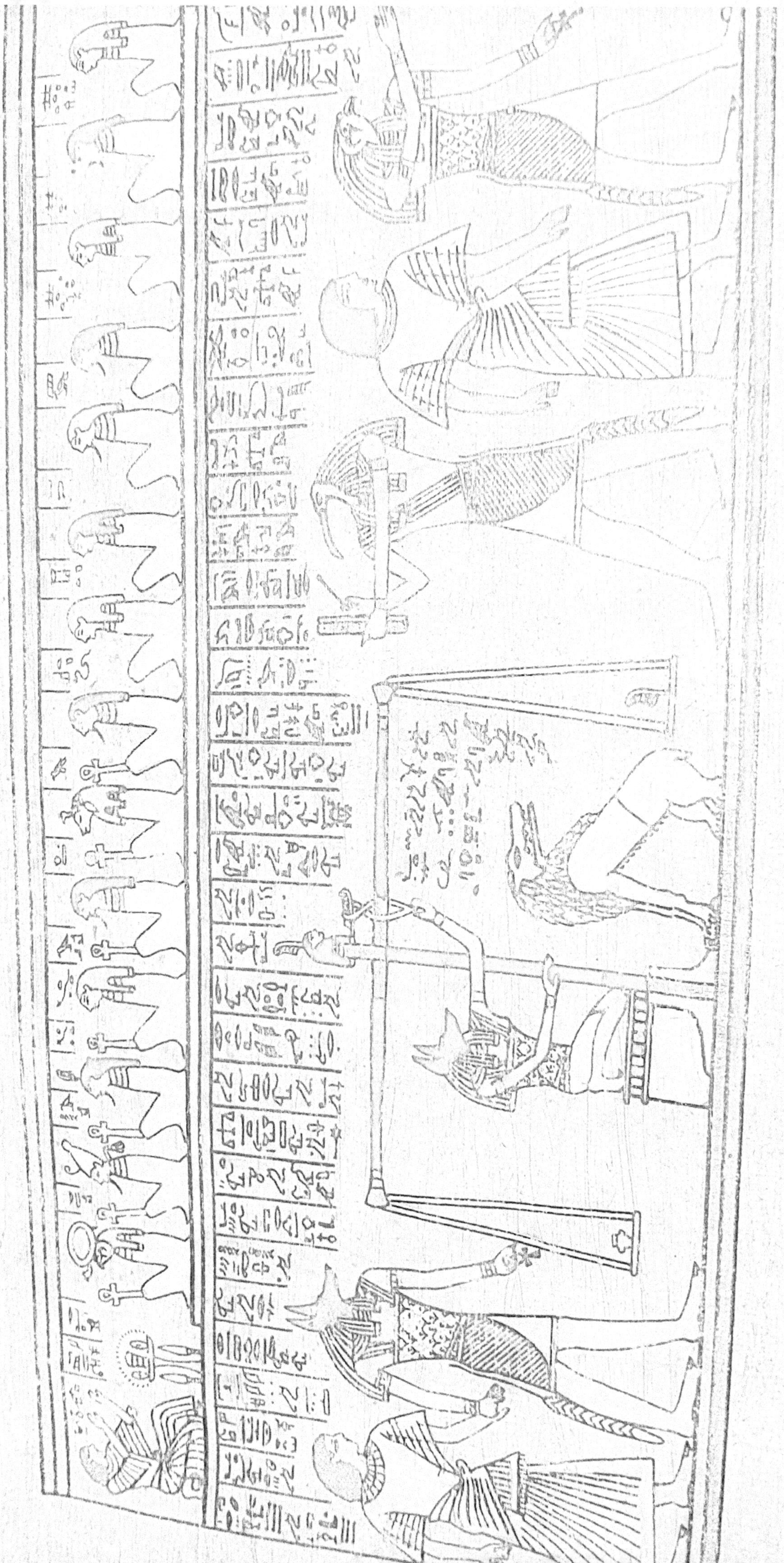

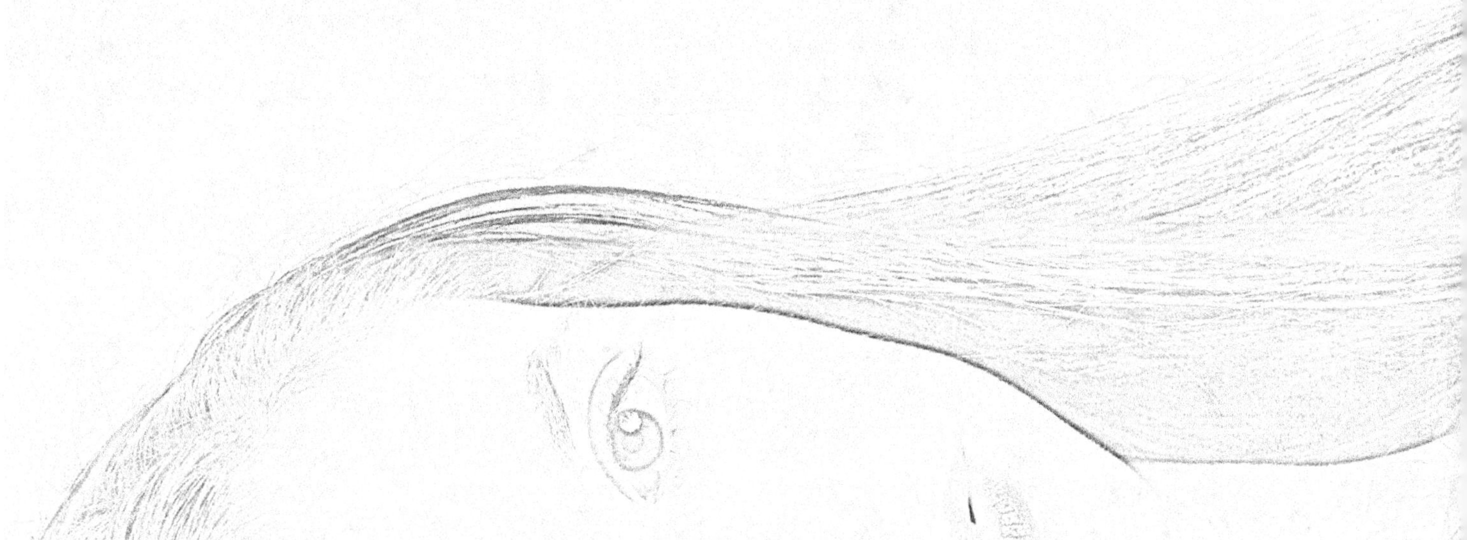

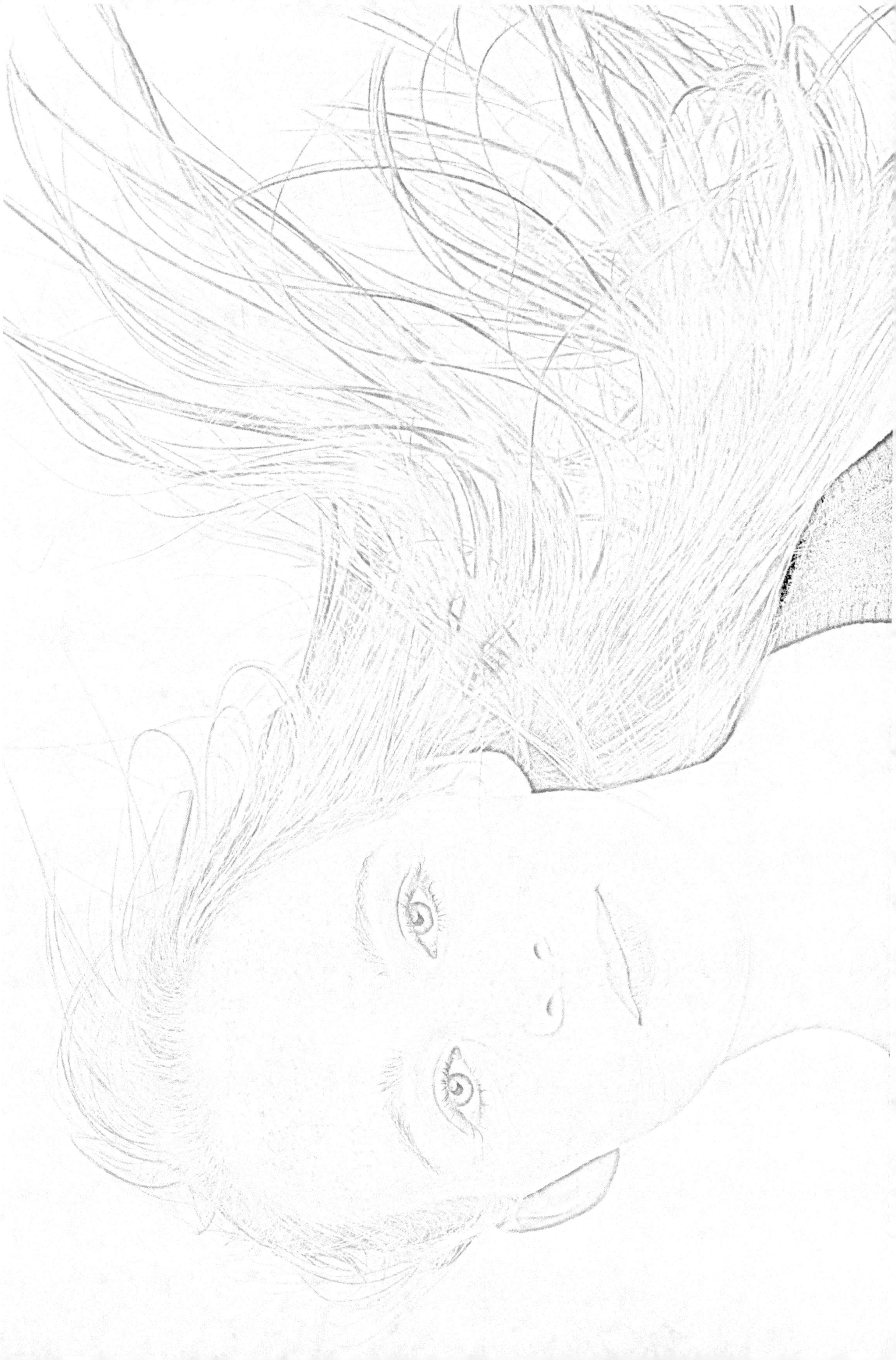

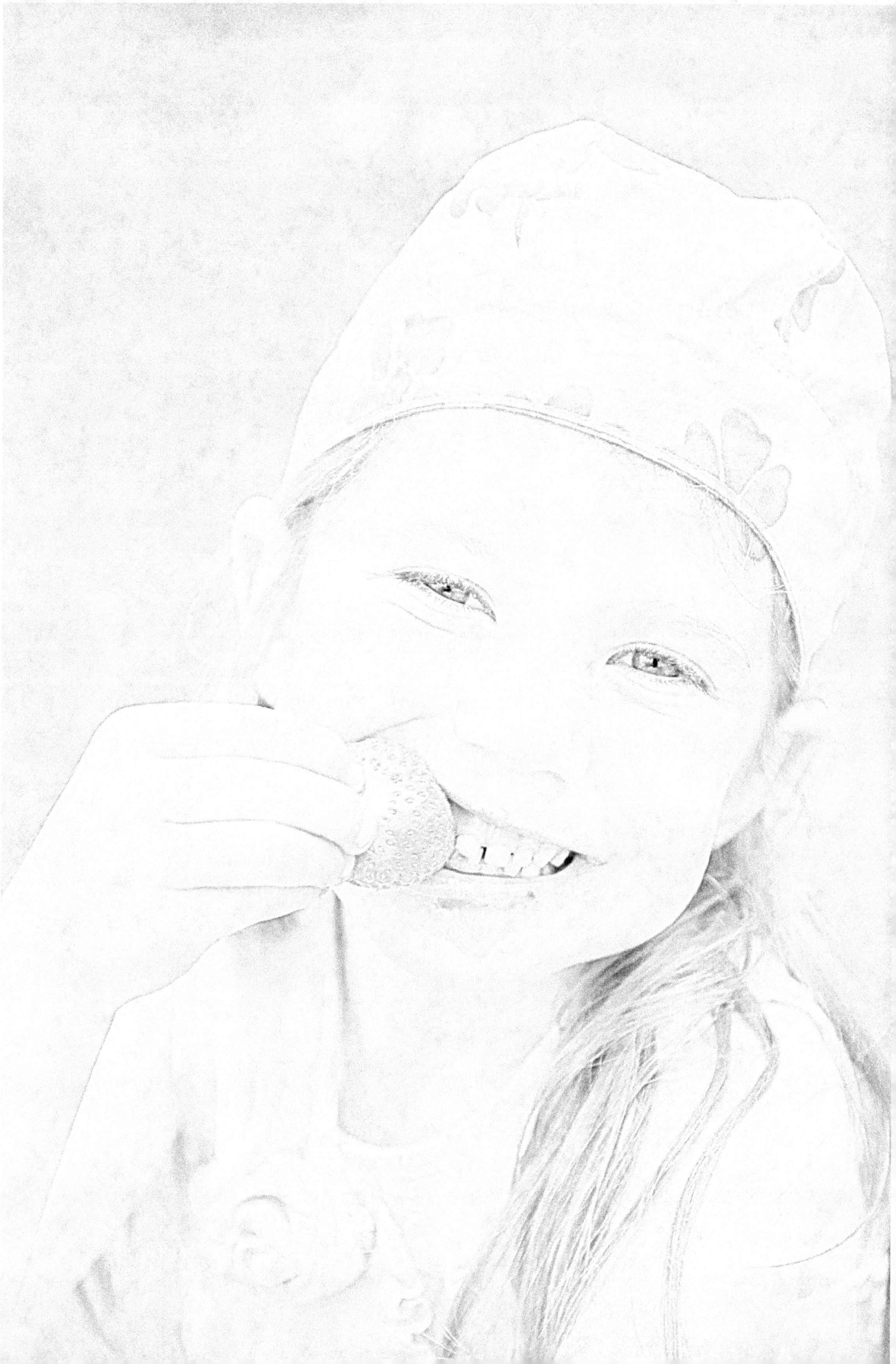

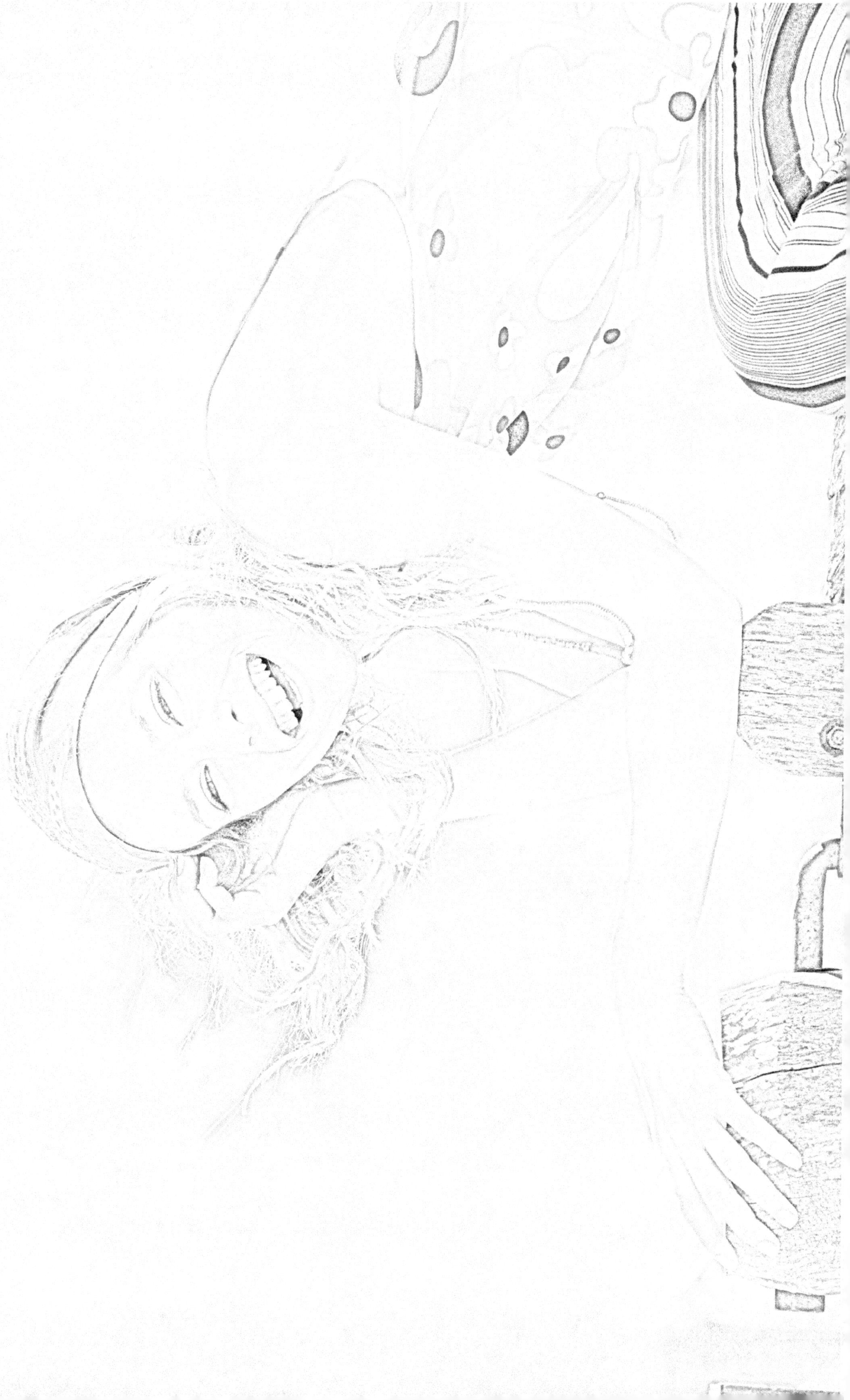

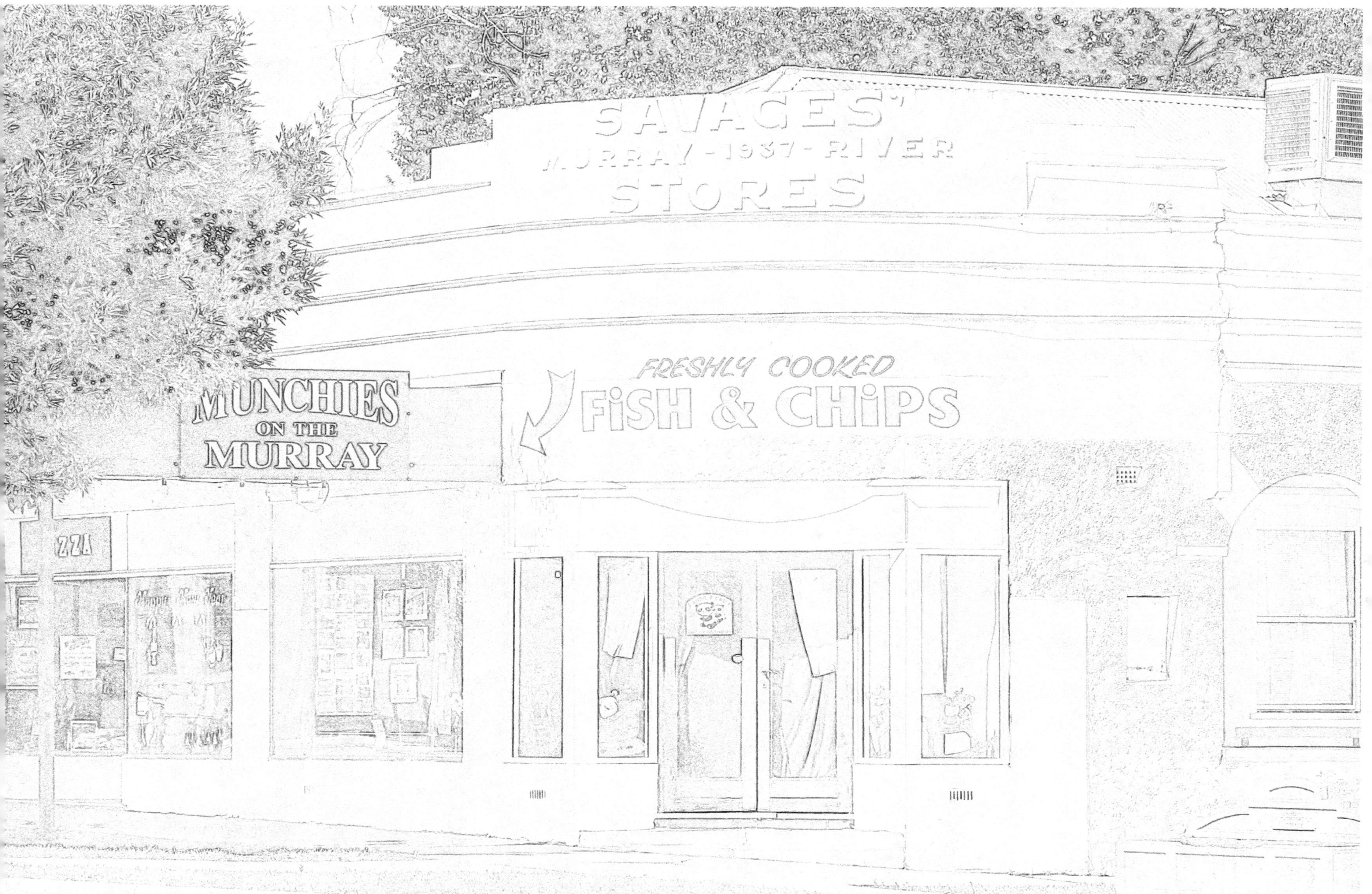
SAVAGES'
MURRAY - 1937 - RIVER
STORES
FRESHLY COOKED
FISH & CHIPS
MUNCHIES
ON THE
MURRAY
22A

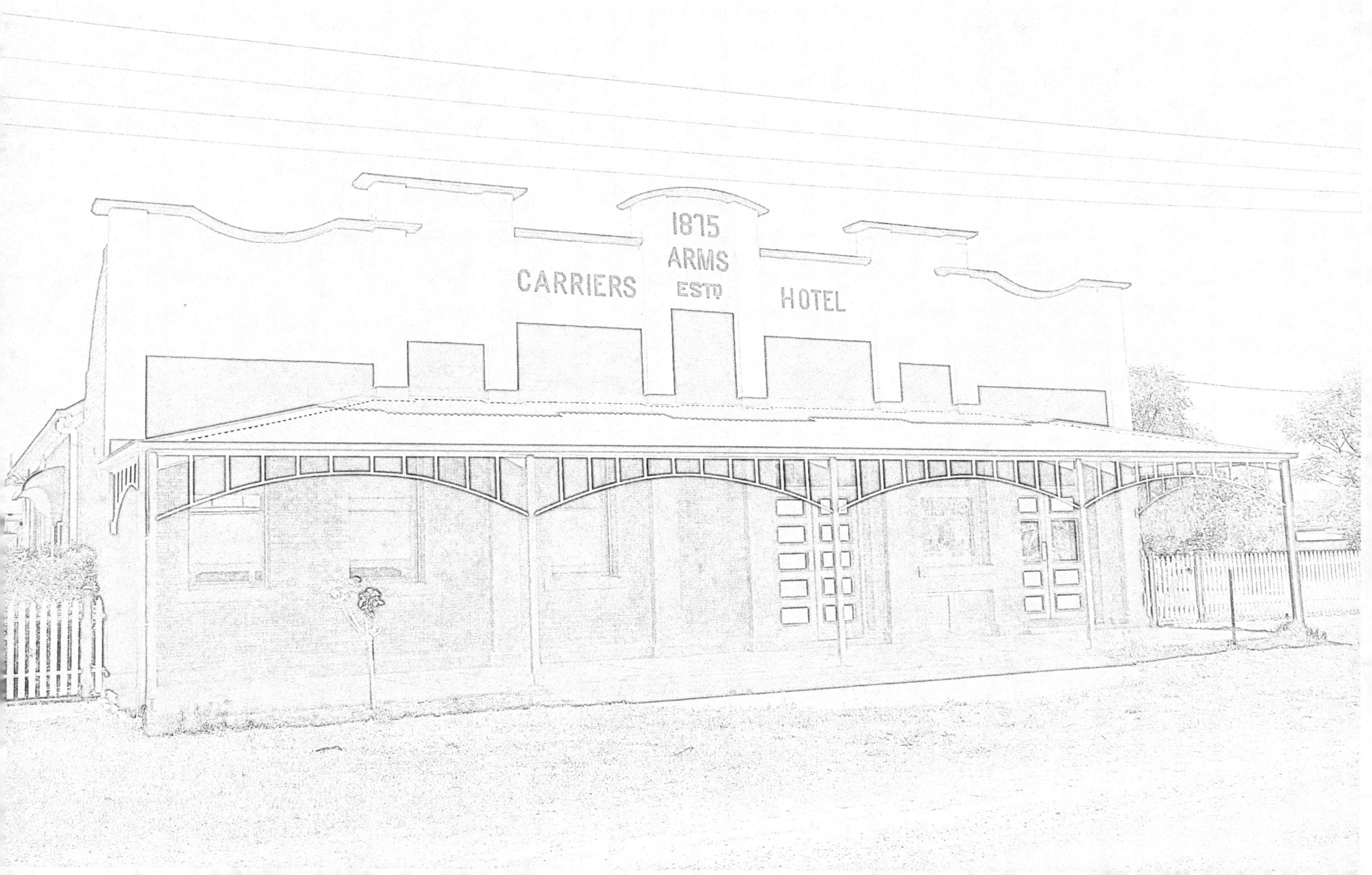
1875
CARRIERS ARMS ESTD HOTEL

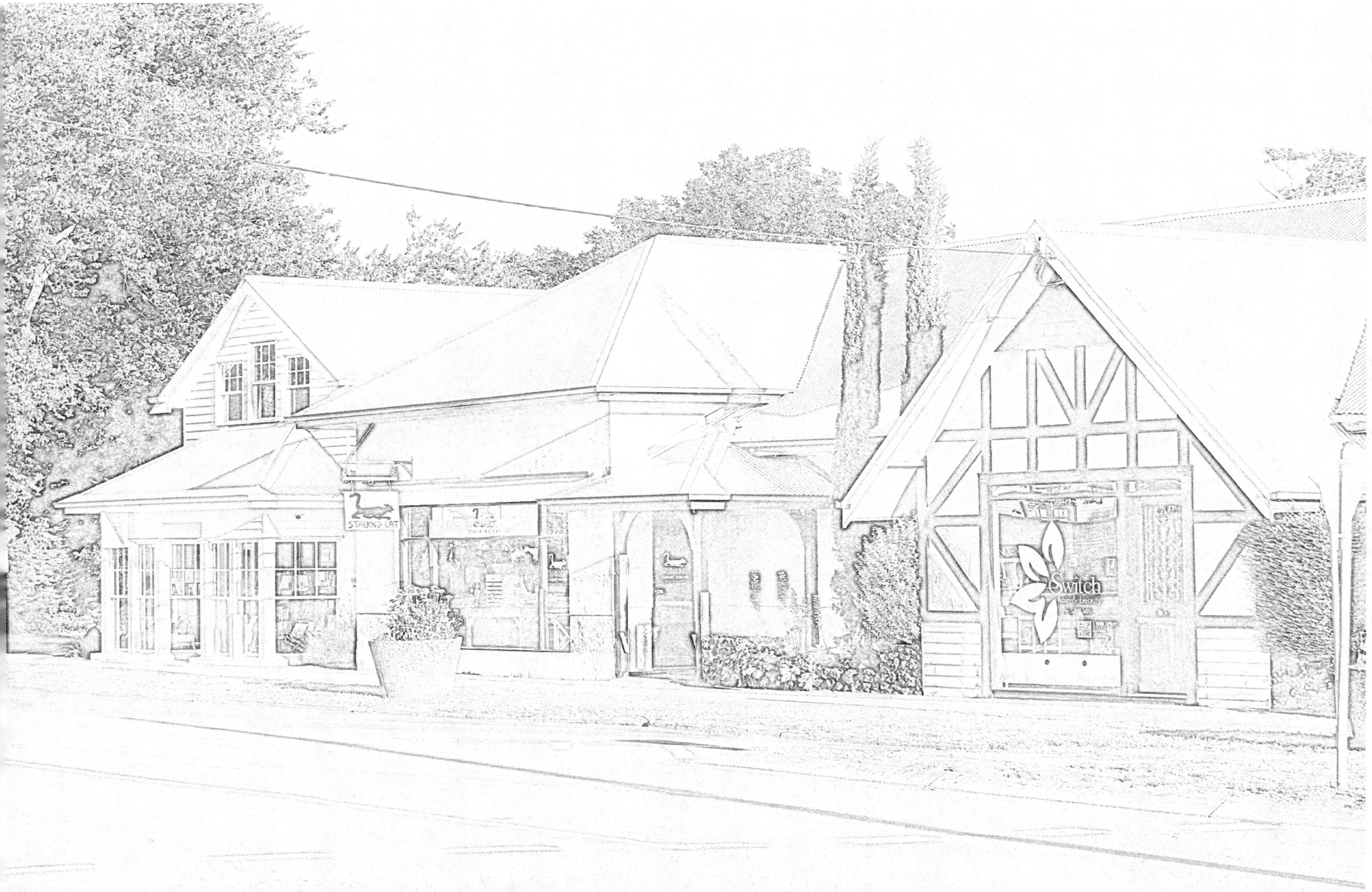
STALKING CAT
Switch

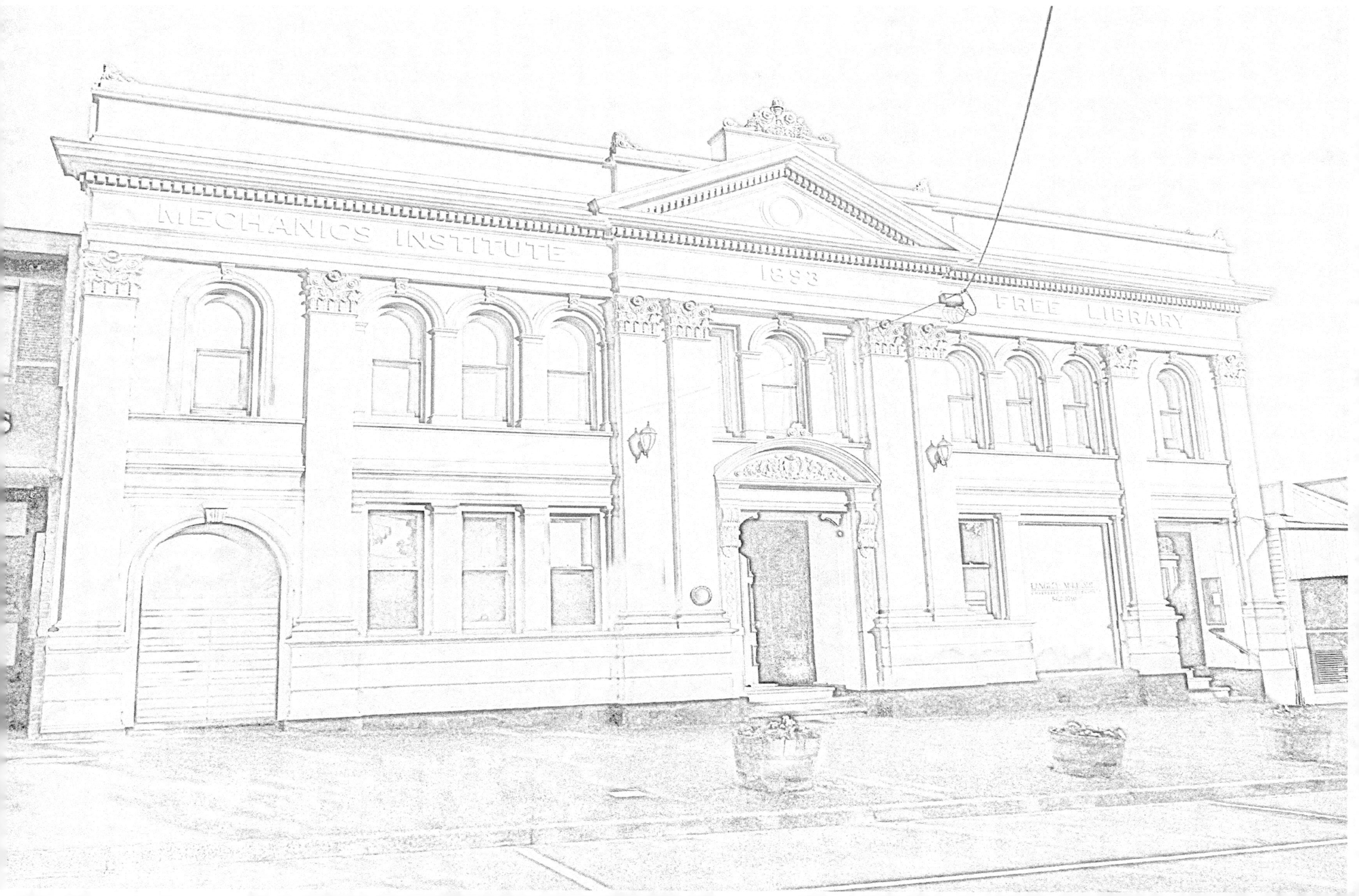
MECHANICS INSTITUTE
1893
FREE LIBRARY

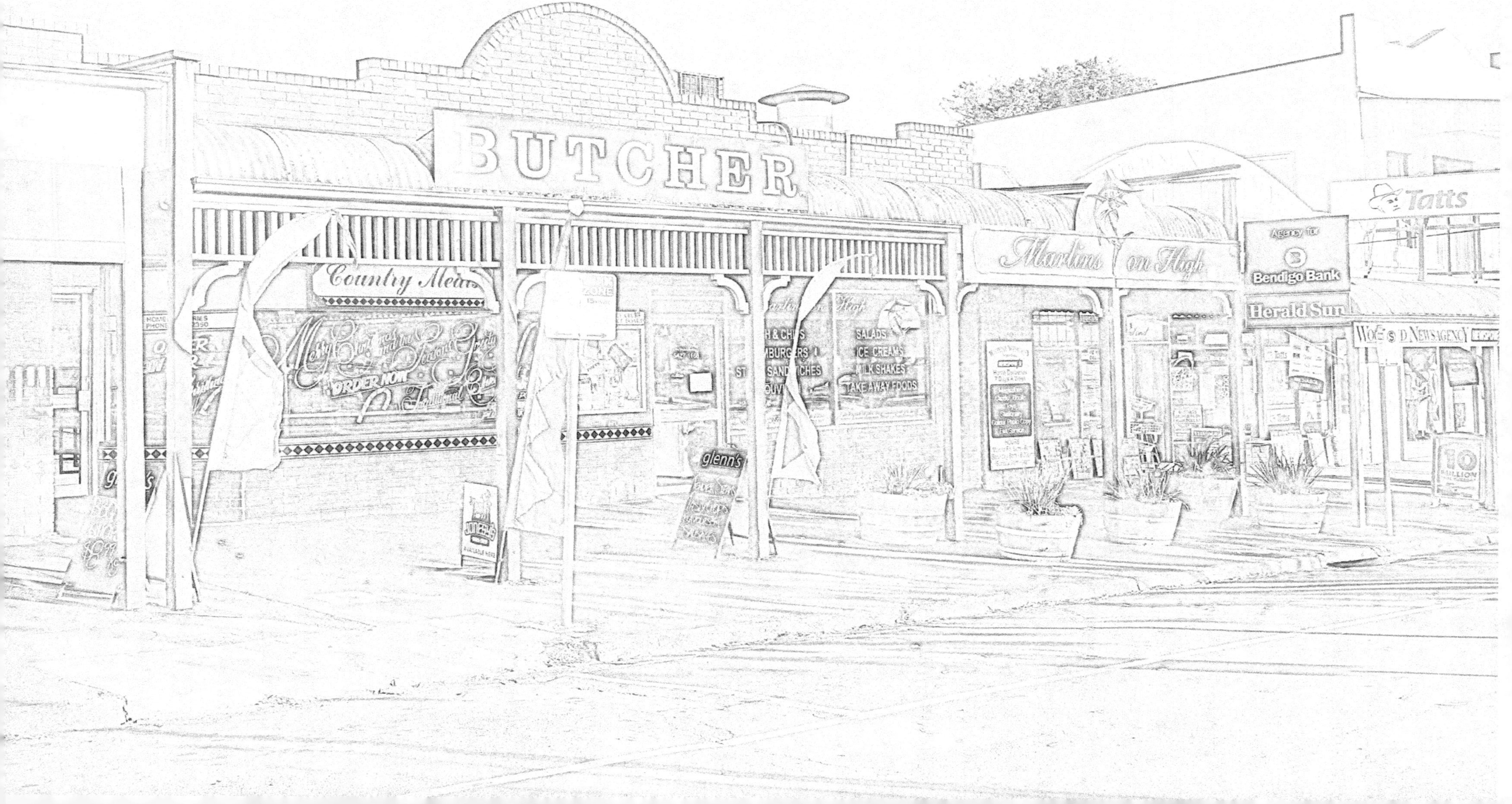
BUTCHER
Country Meats
ORDER NOW
SALADS
ICE CREAMS
MILK SHAKES
TAKE AWAY FOODS
glenn's
Martins on High
Agency for
Bendigo Bank
Herald Sun
Tatts

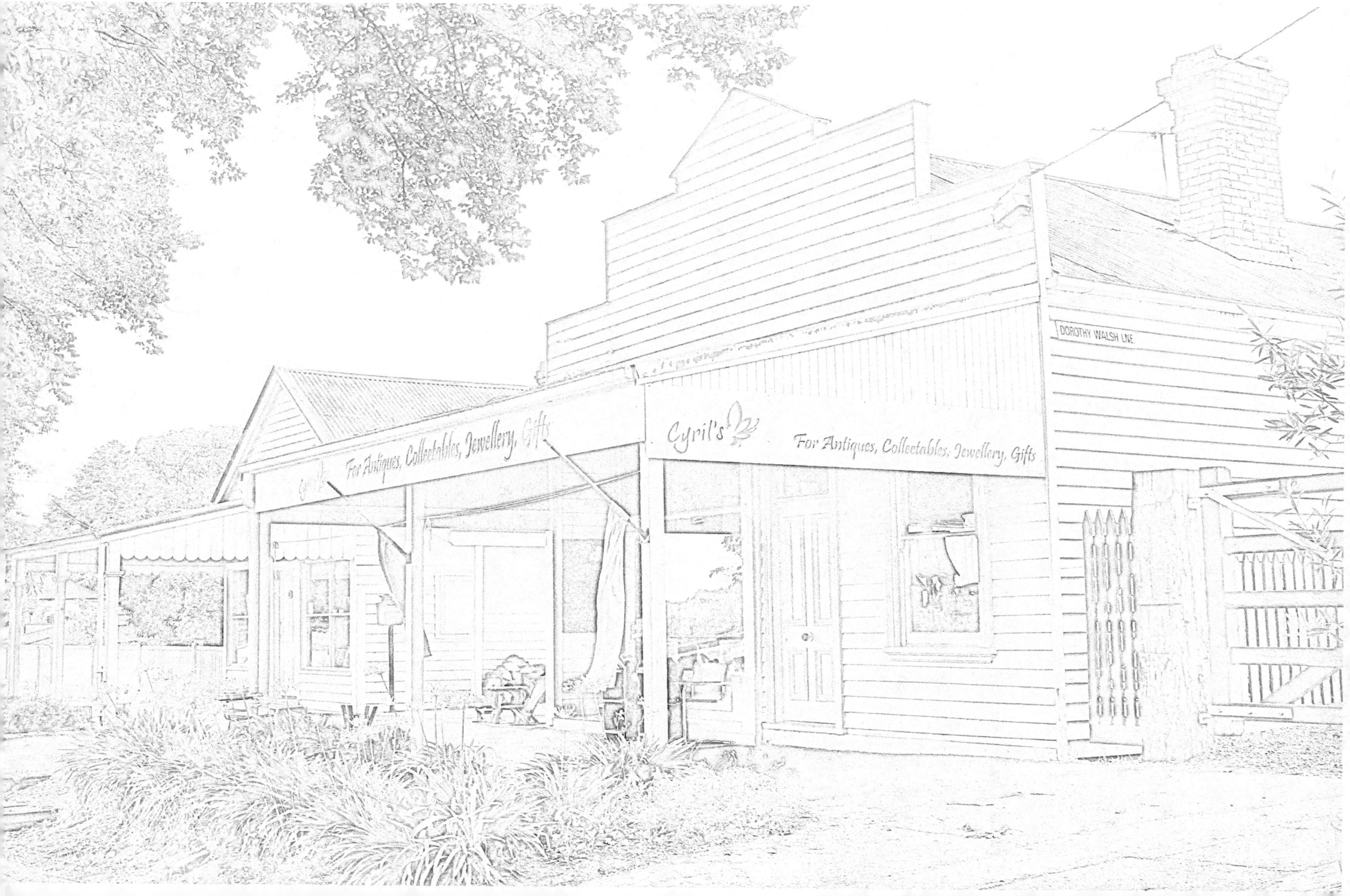
For Antiques, Collectables, Jewellery, Gifts
Cyril's
For Antiques, Collectables, Jewellery, Gifts
DOROTHY WALSH LNE

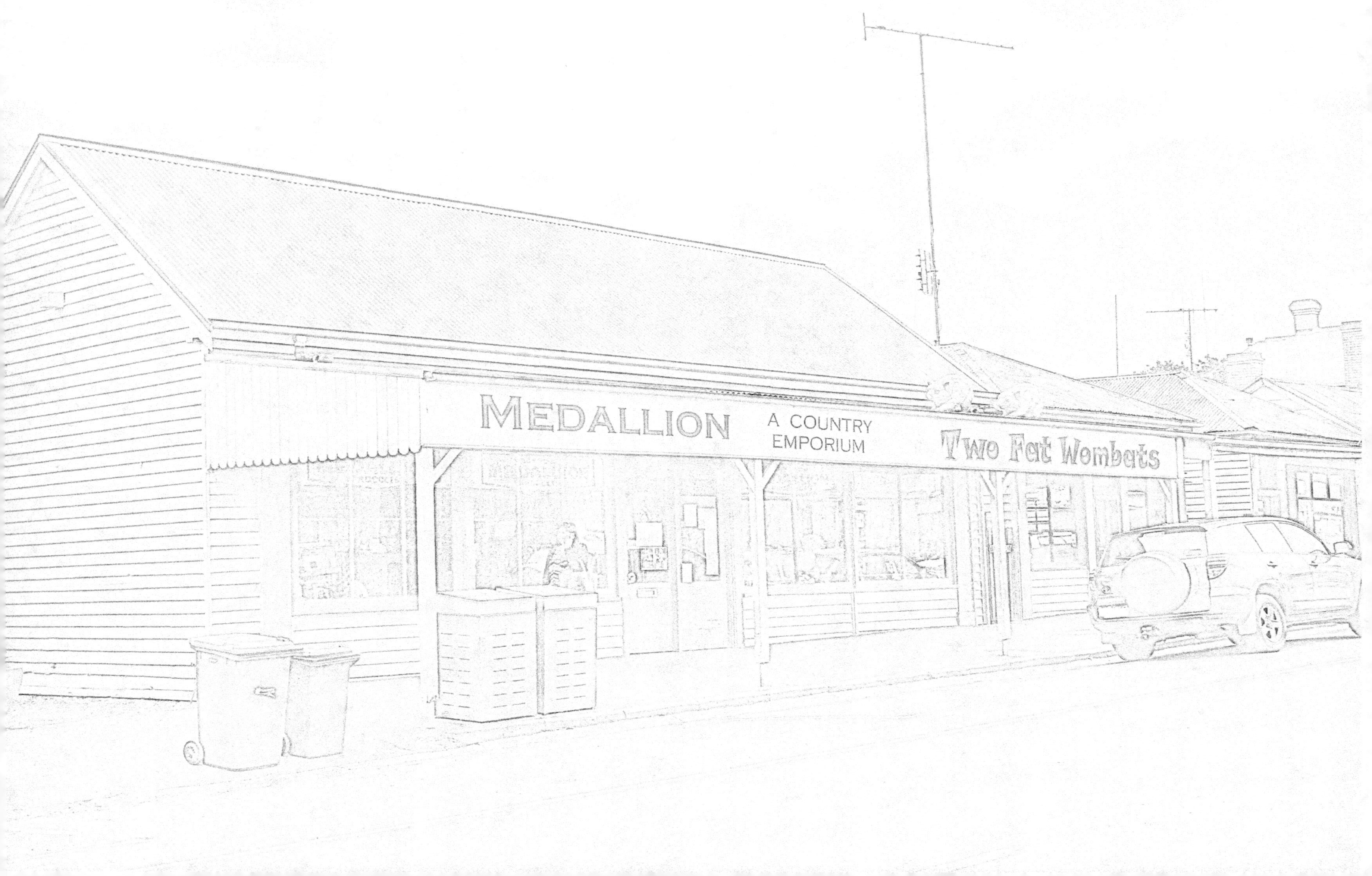
MEDALLION
A COUNTRY EMPORIUM
Two Fat Wombats

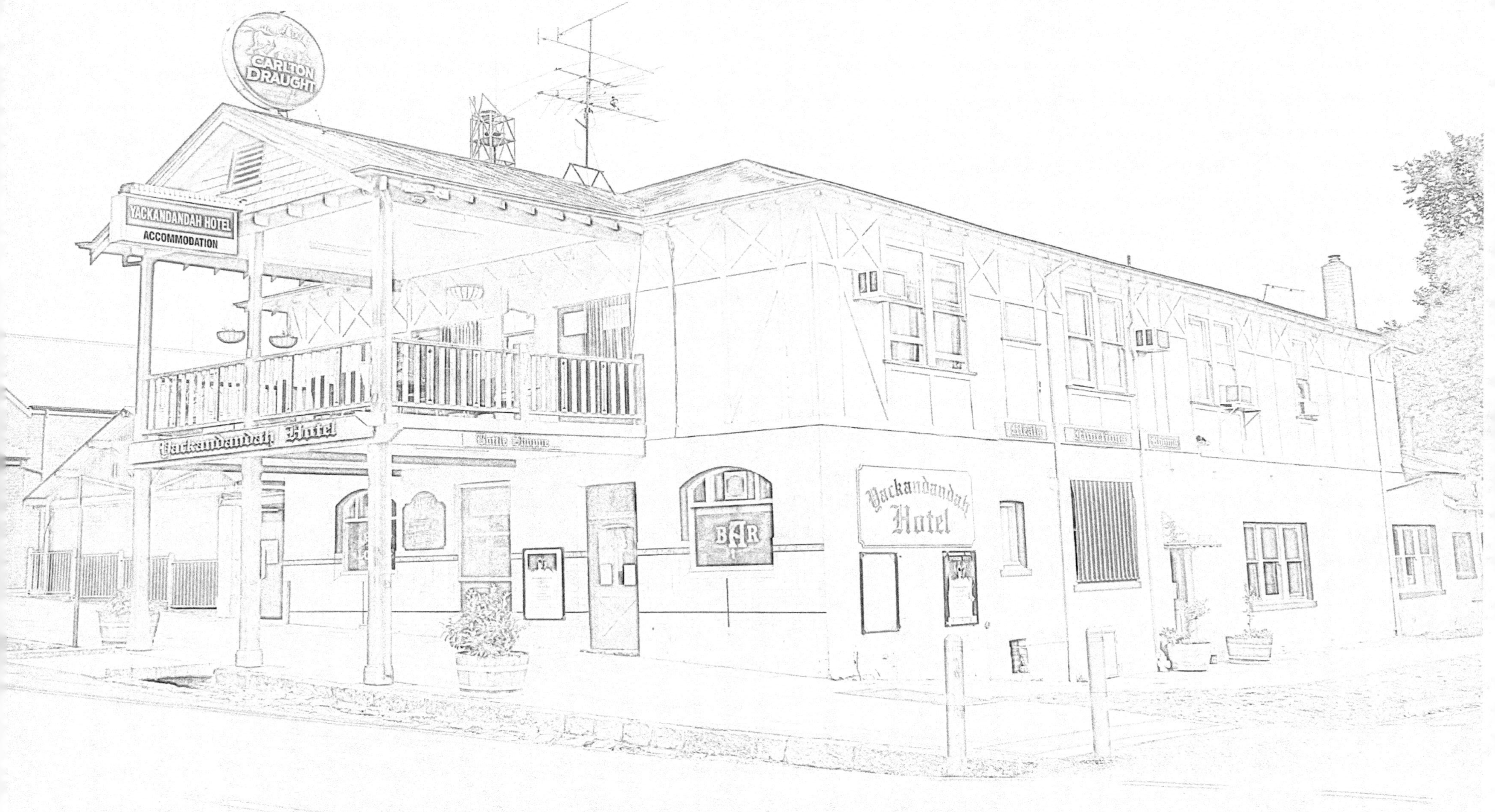
CARLTON DRAUGHT
YACKANDANDAH HOTEL
ACCOMMODATION
Yackandandah Hotel
Bottle Shoppe
BAR
Yackandandah Hotel

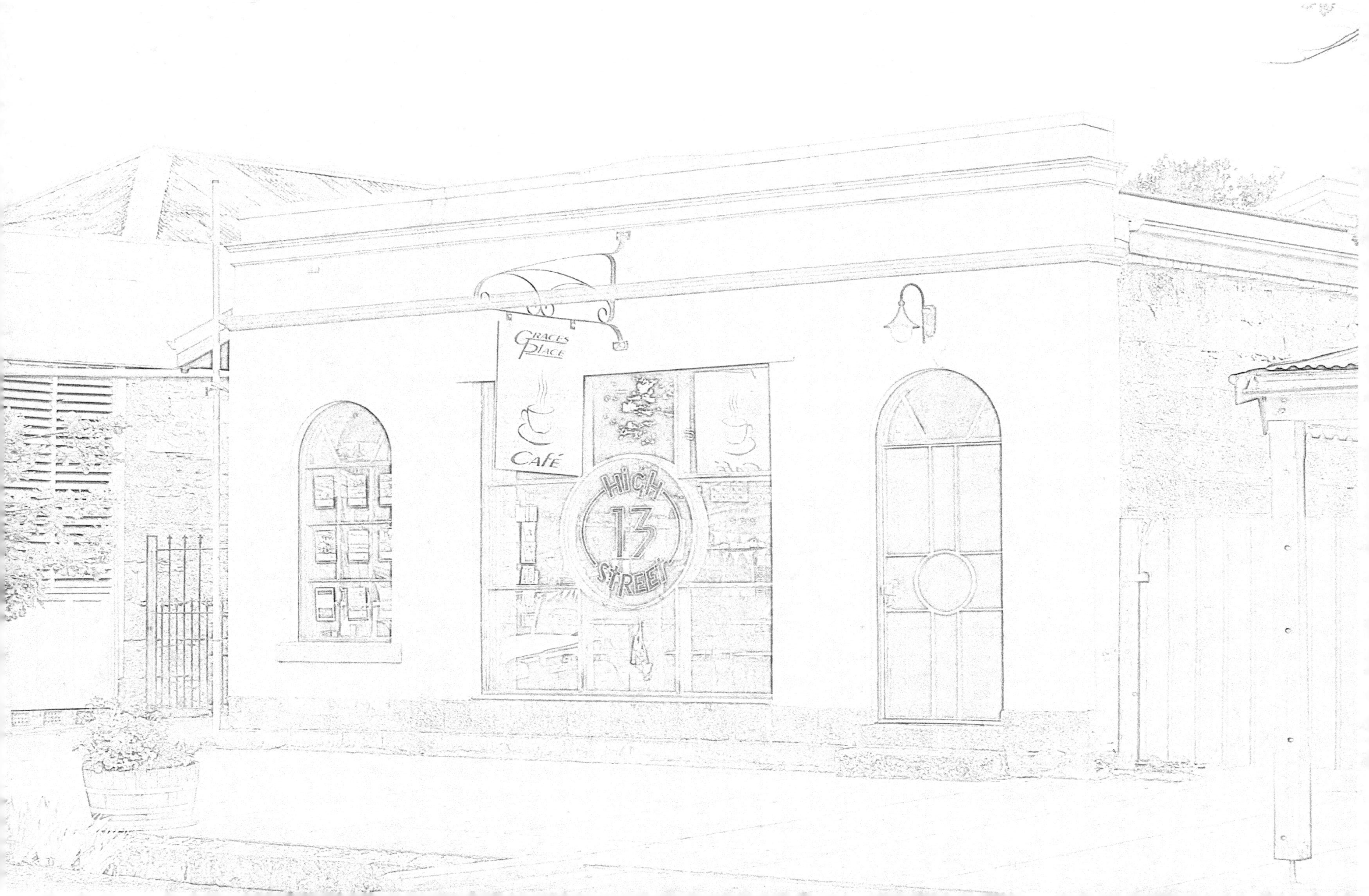
GRACES PLACE
CAFÉ
HIGH
13
STREET

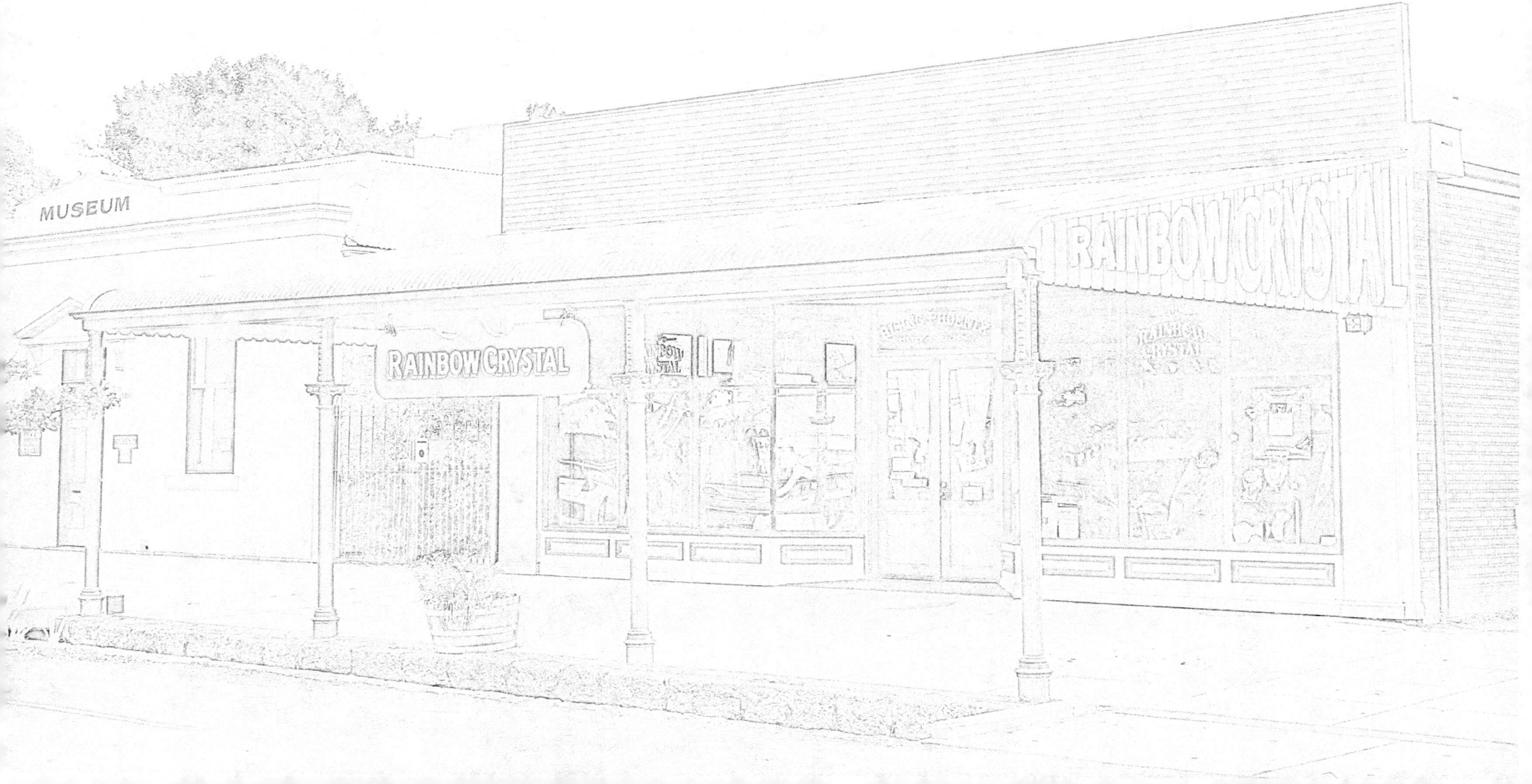
MUSEUM
RAINBOW CRYSTAL
RAINBOW CRYSTAL

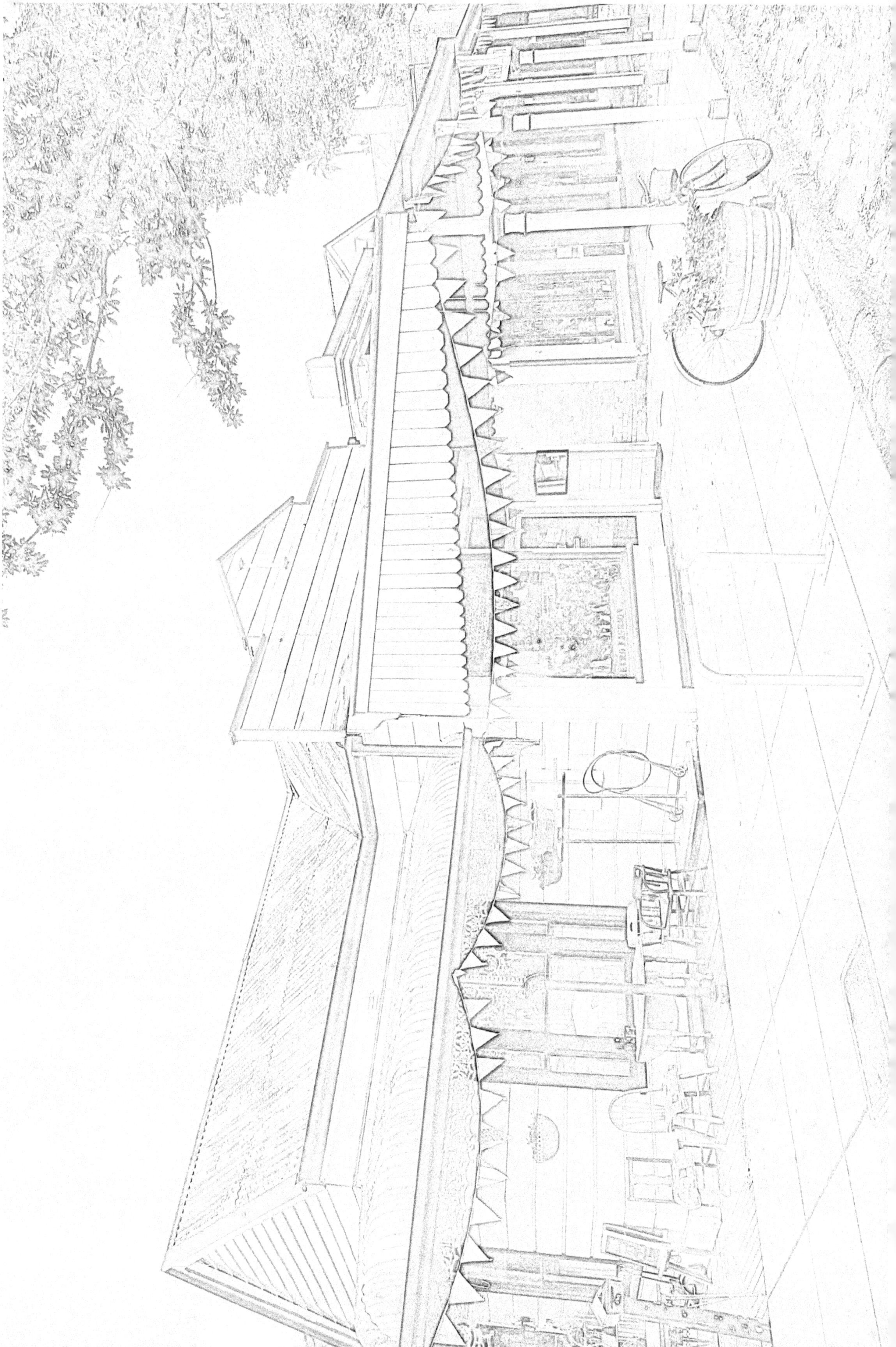

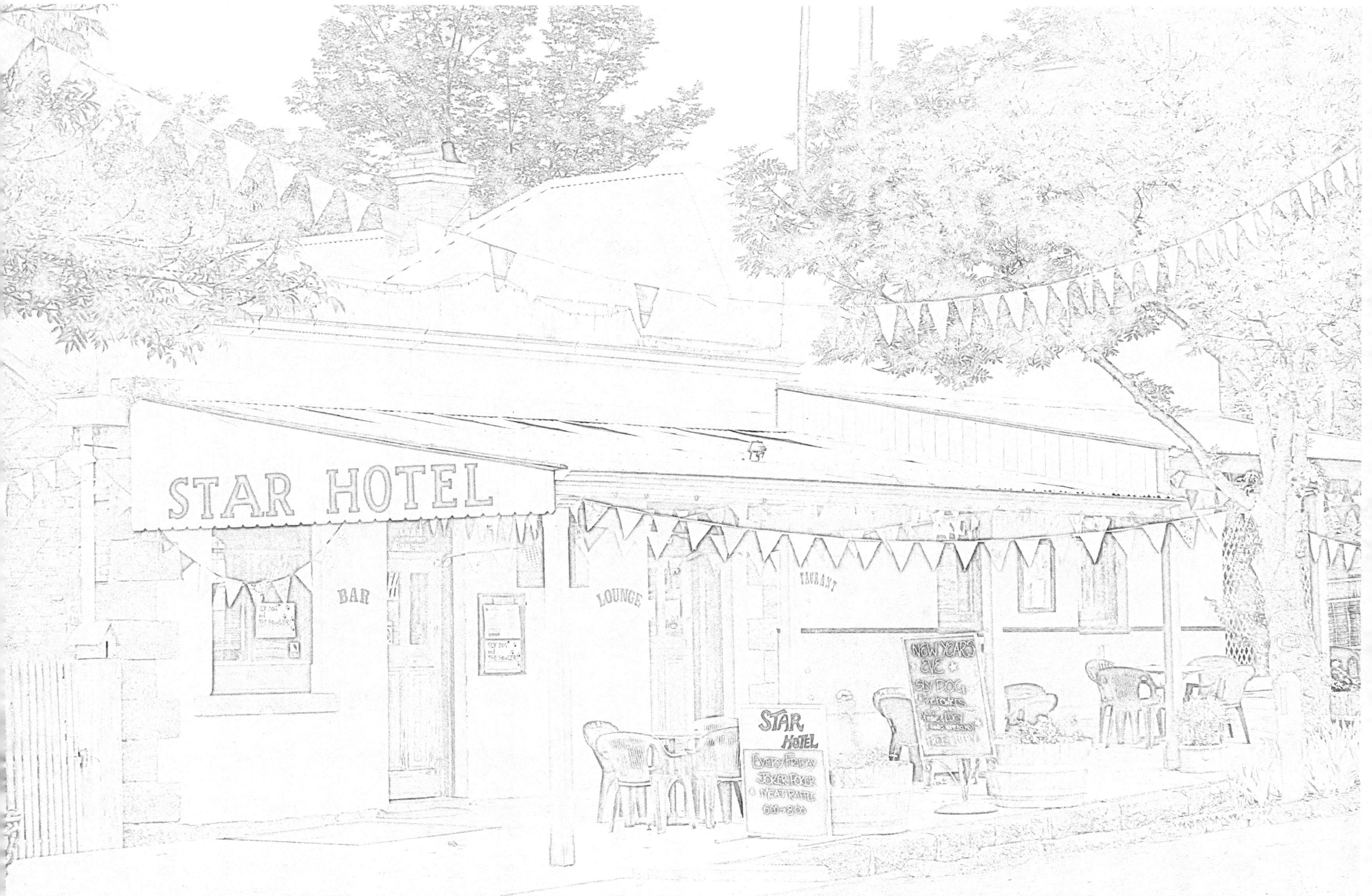
STAR HOTEL
BAR
LOUNGE
NEW YEARS EVE
STAR HOTEL
EVERY FRIDAY
JOKER POKER
& MEAT RAFFLE

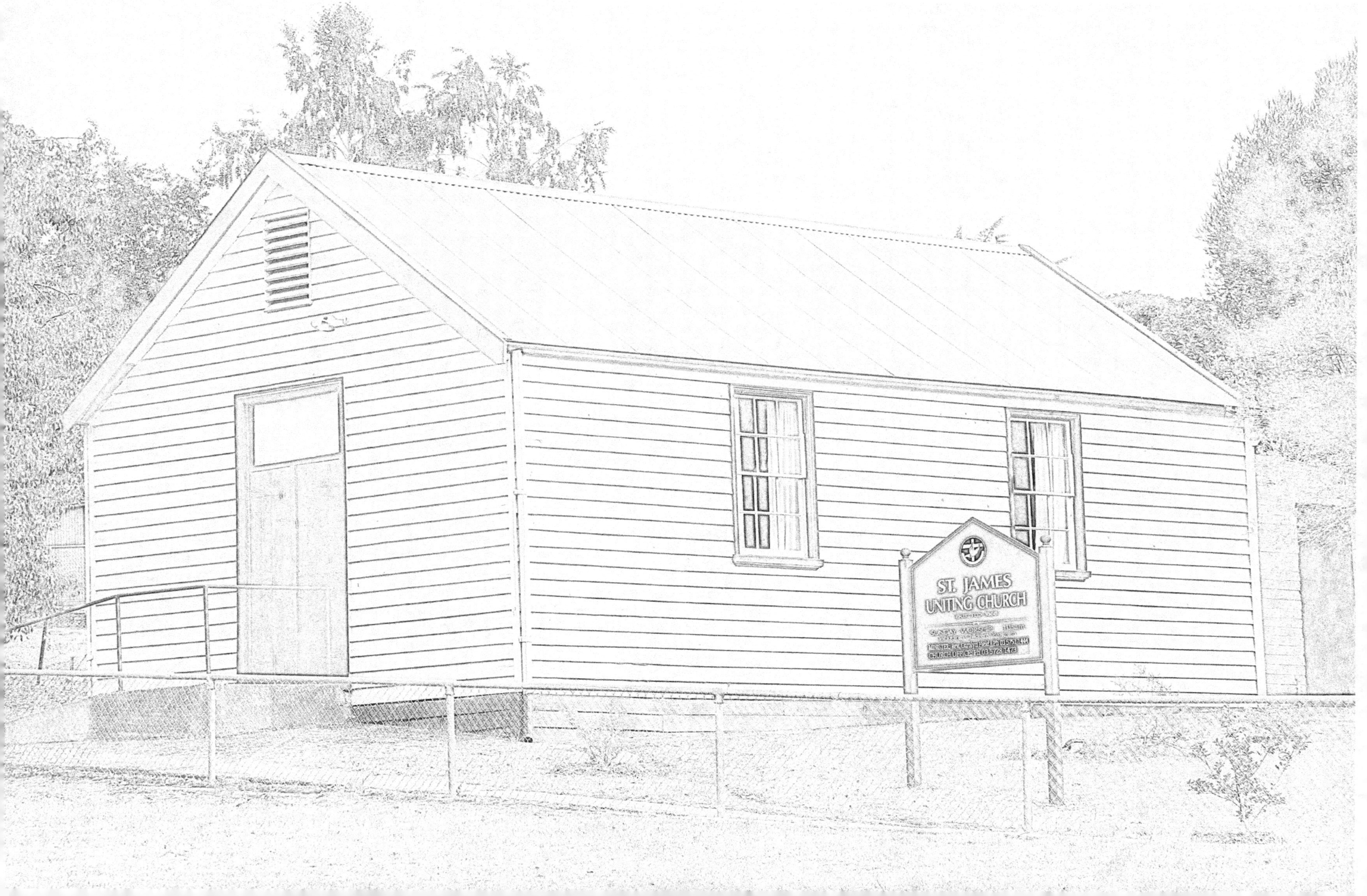
ST. JAMES
UNITING CHURCH
SUNDAY WORSHIP

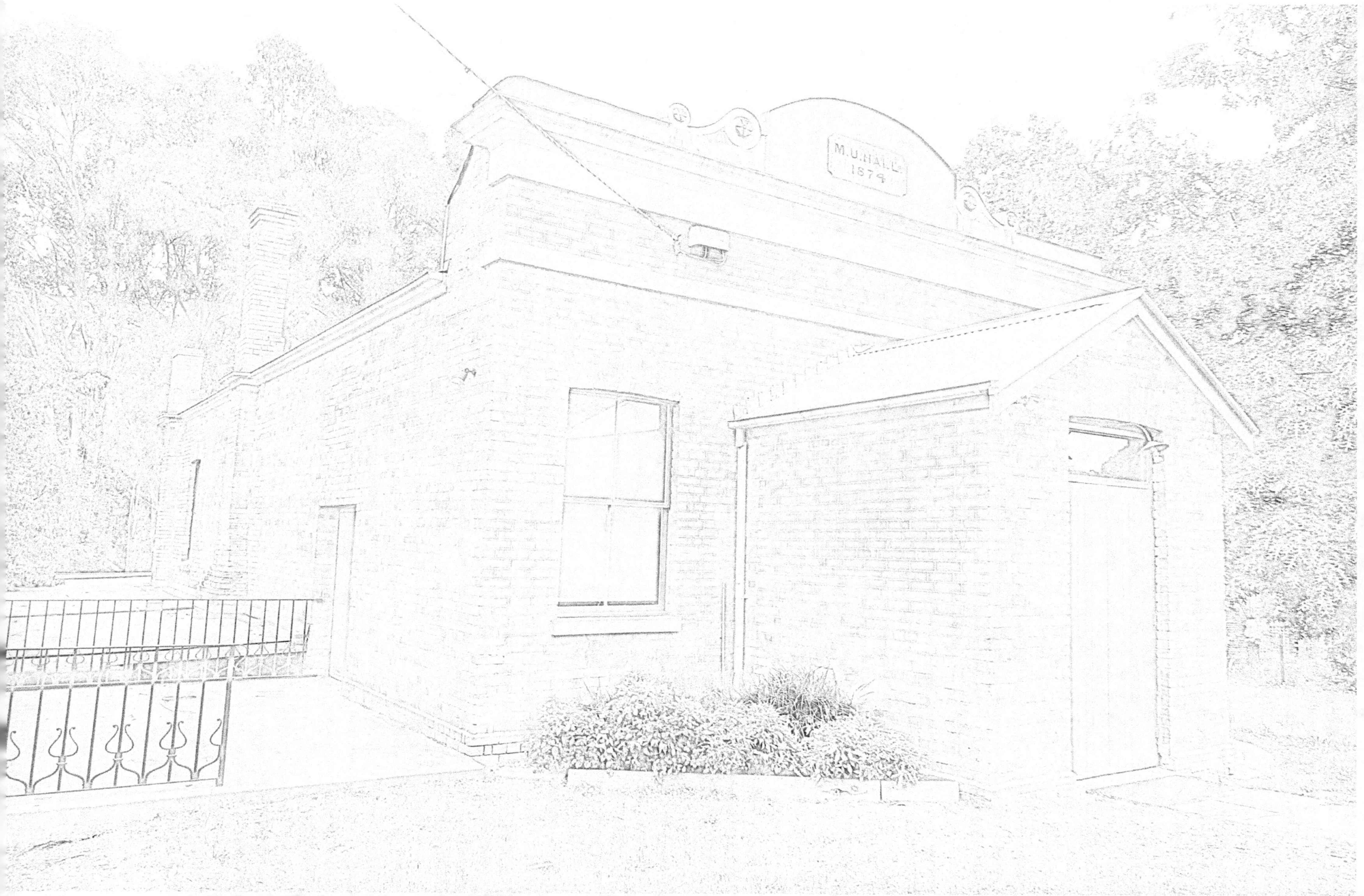
M.U.HALL
1874

CARLTON DRAUGHT
WESTERN HOTEL
WICKIE BAR
WESTERN HOTEL
WICKIE LOUNGE

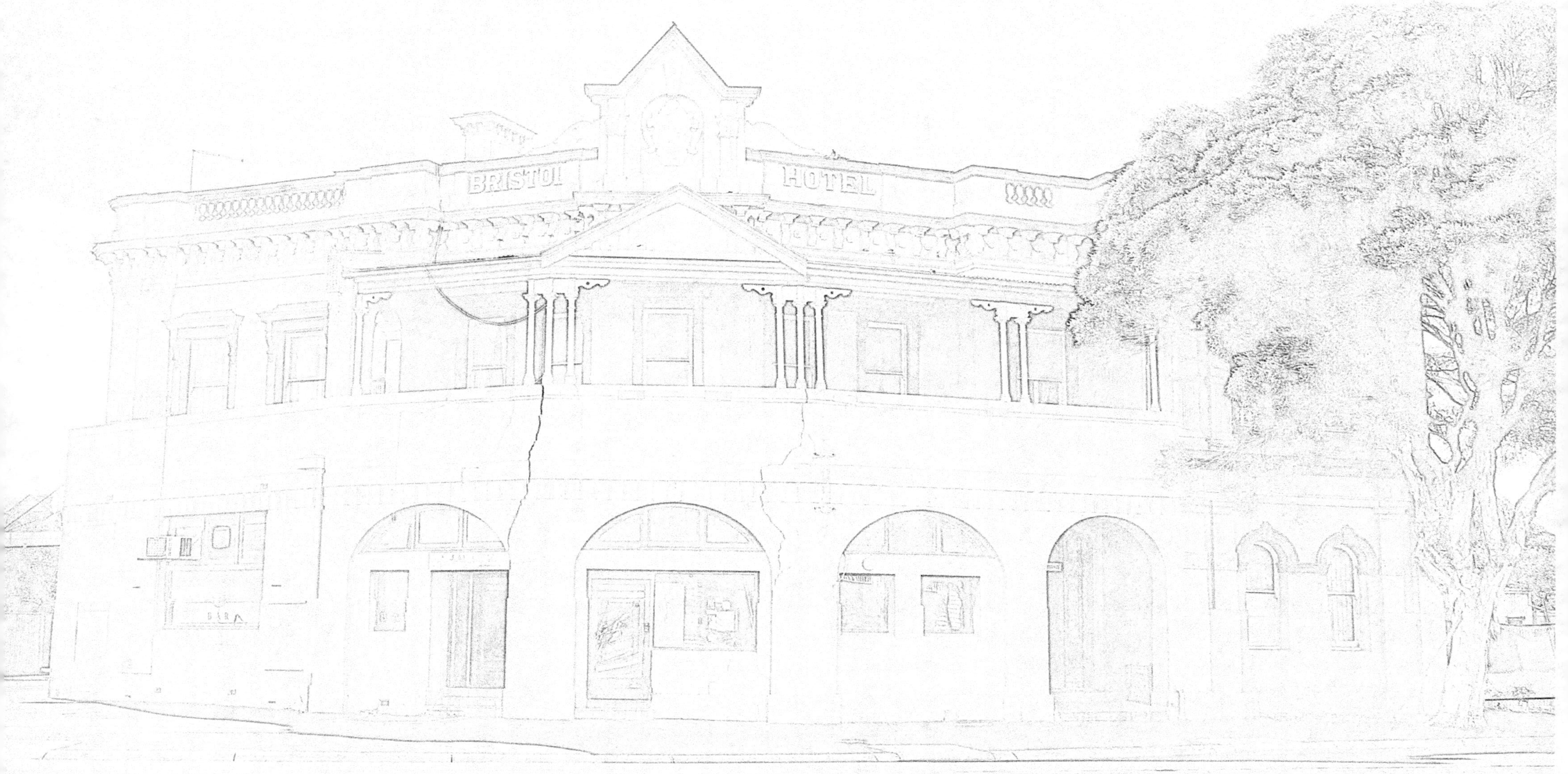
BRISTOL
HOTEL

WILLIAMSTOWN R.S.L
WAY OUT WEST
ROOTS MUSIC CLUB

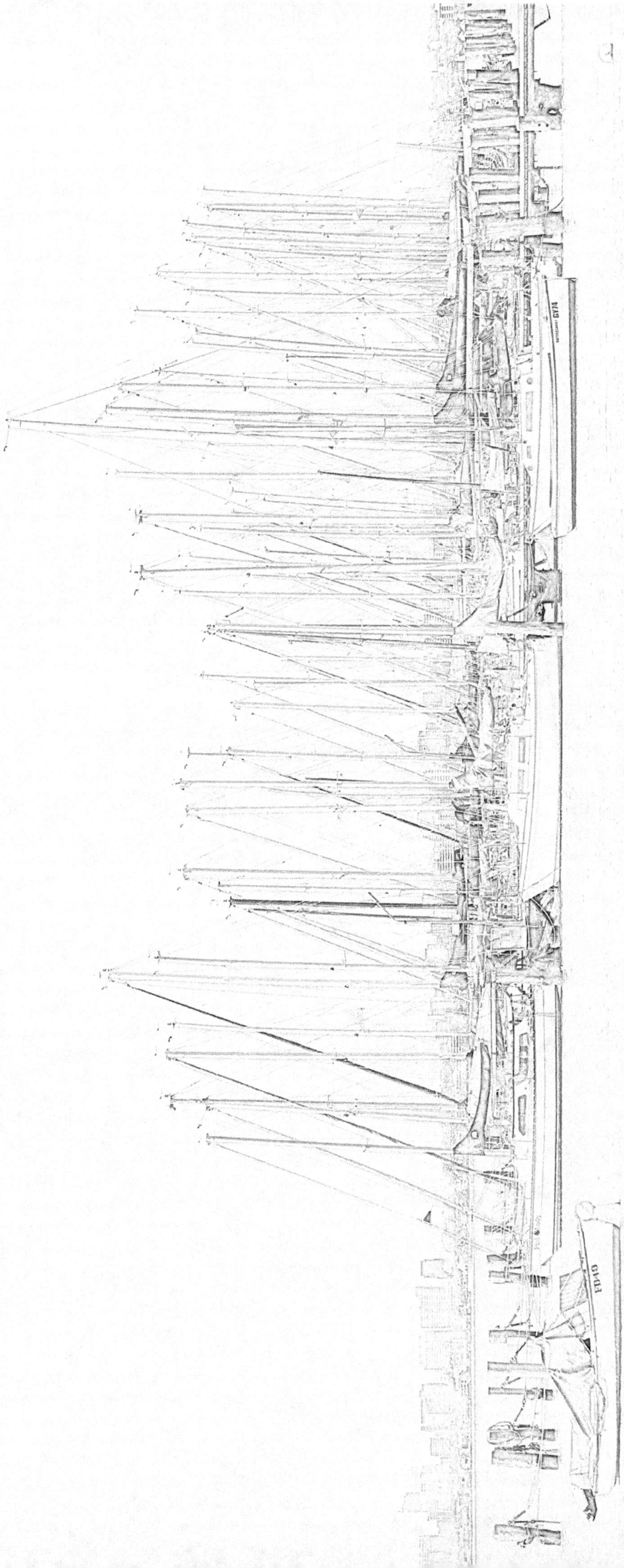
GY74
FD49

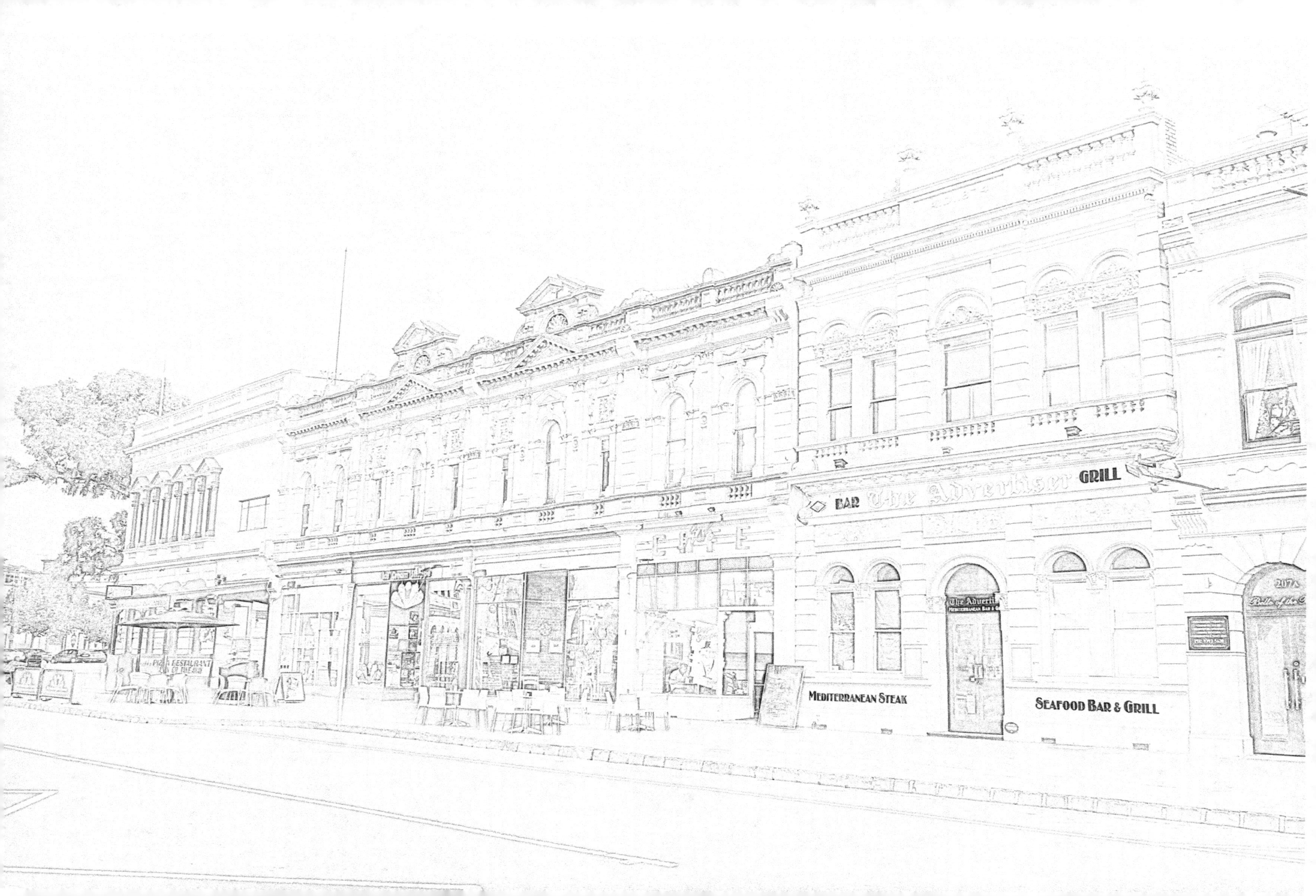
BAR The Advertiser GRILL
CAFE
MEDITERRANEAN STEAK
SEAFOOD BAR & GRILL
PIZZA RESTAURANT

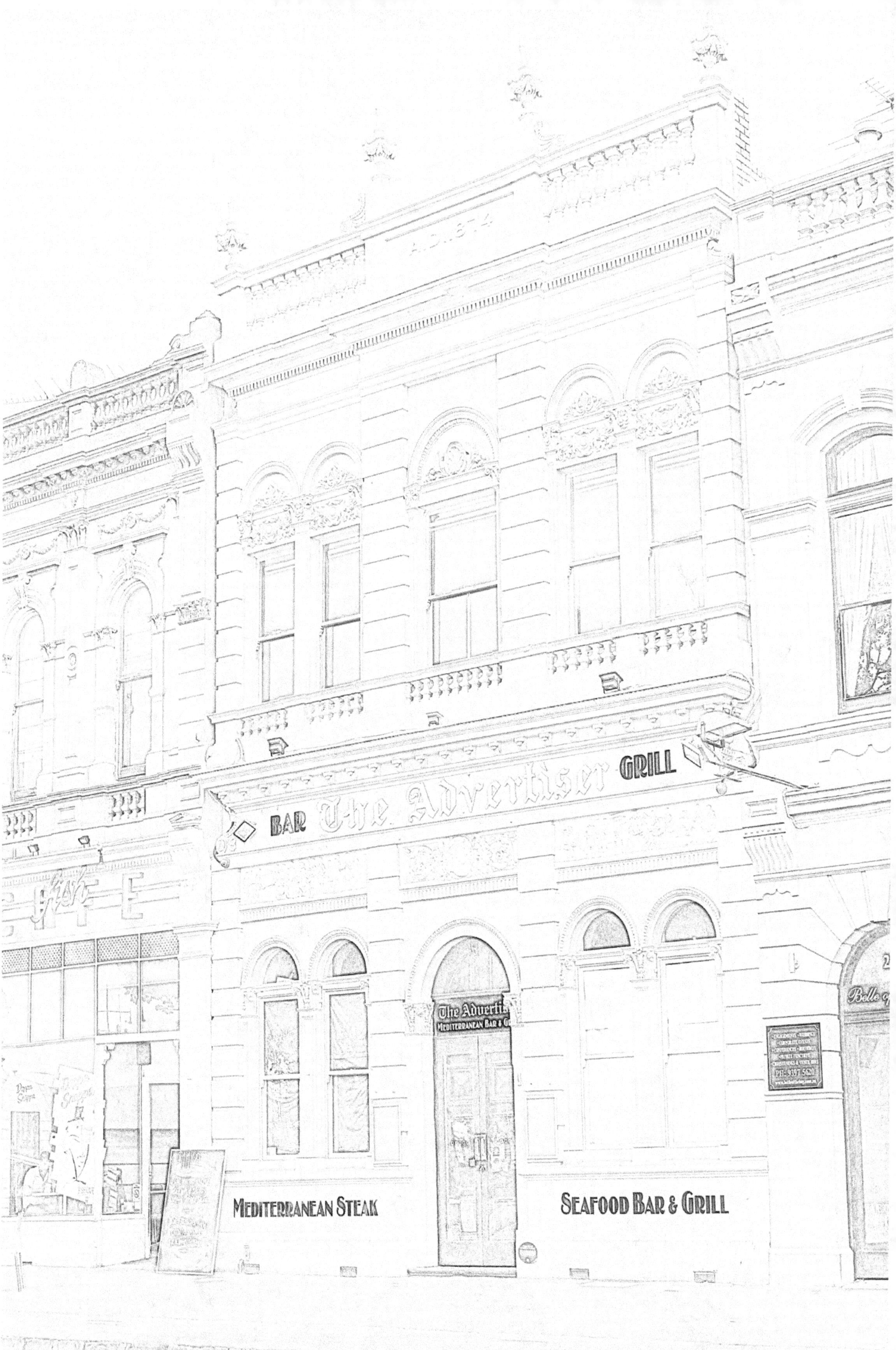
BAR
The Advertiser
GRILL
MEDITERRANEAN STEAK
SEAFOOD BAR & GRILL

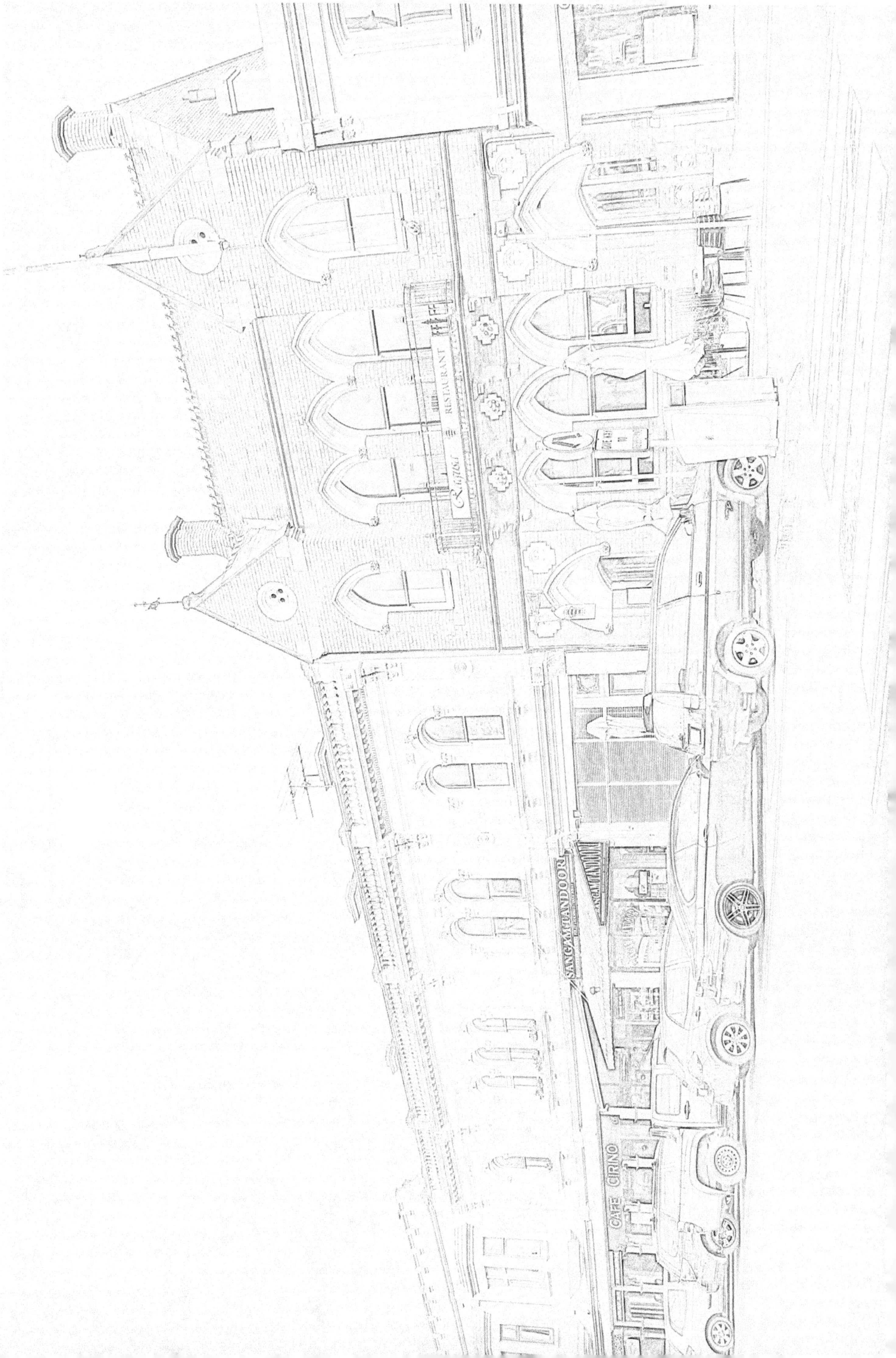
RESTAURANT
SANGAM TANDOOR
CAFE CIRINO

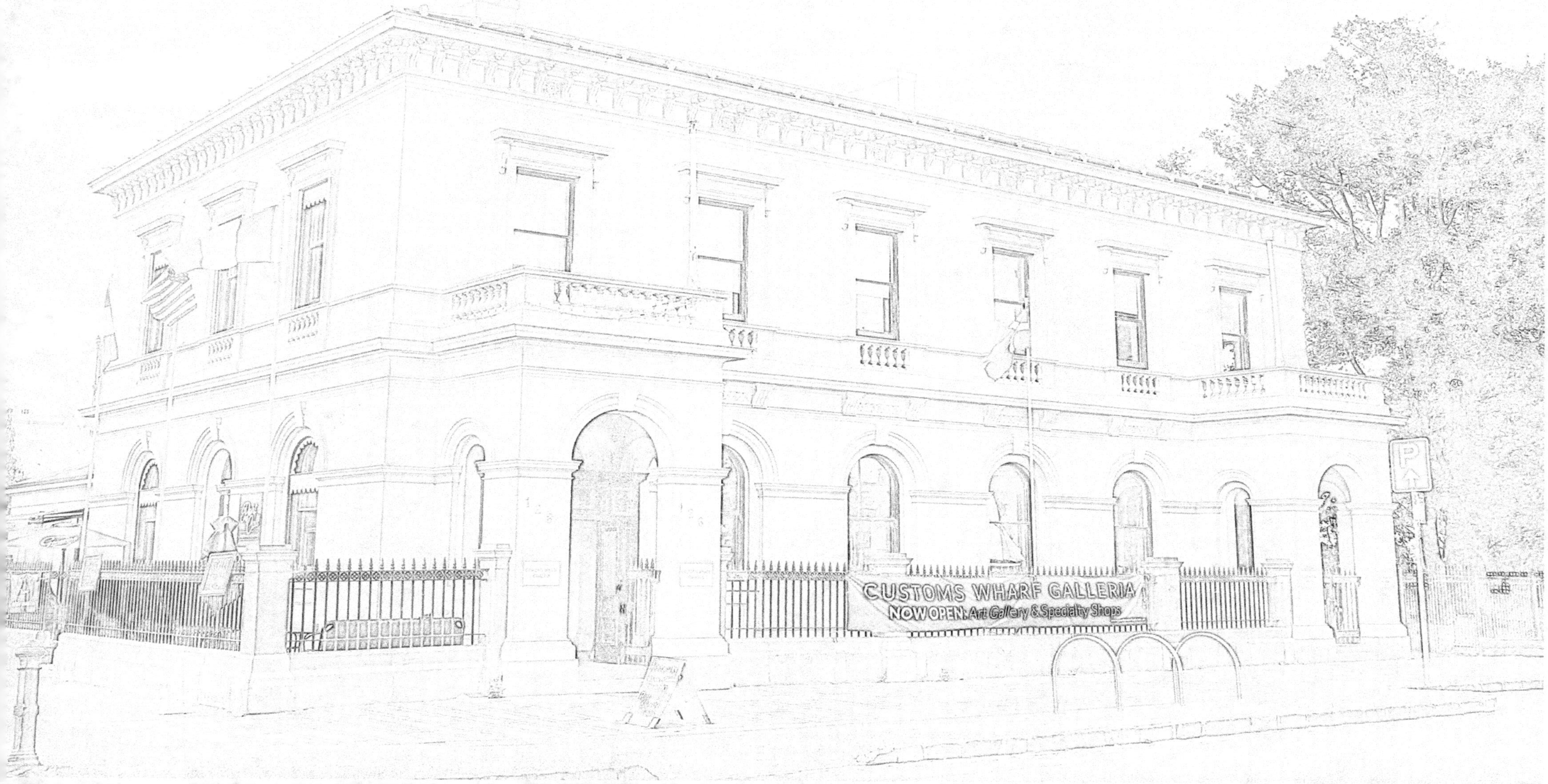
CUSTOMS WHARF GALLERIA
NOW OPEN: Art Gallery & Specialty Shops
P

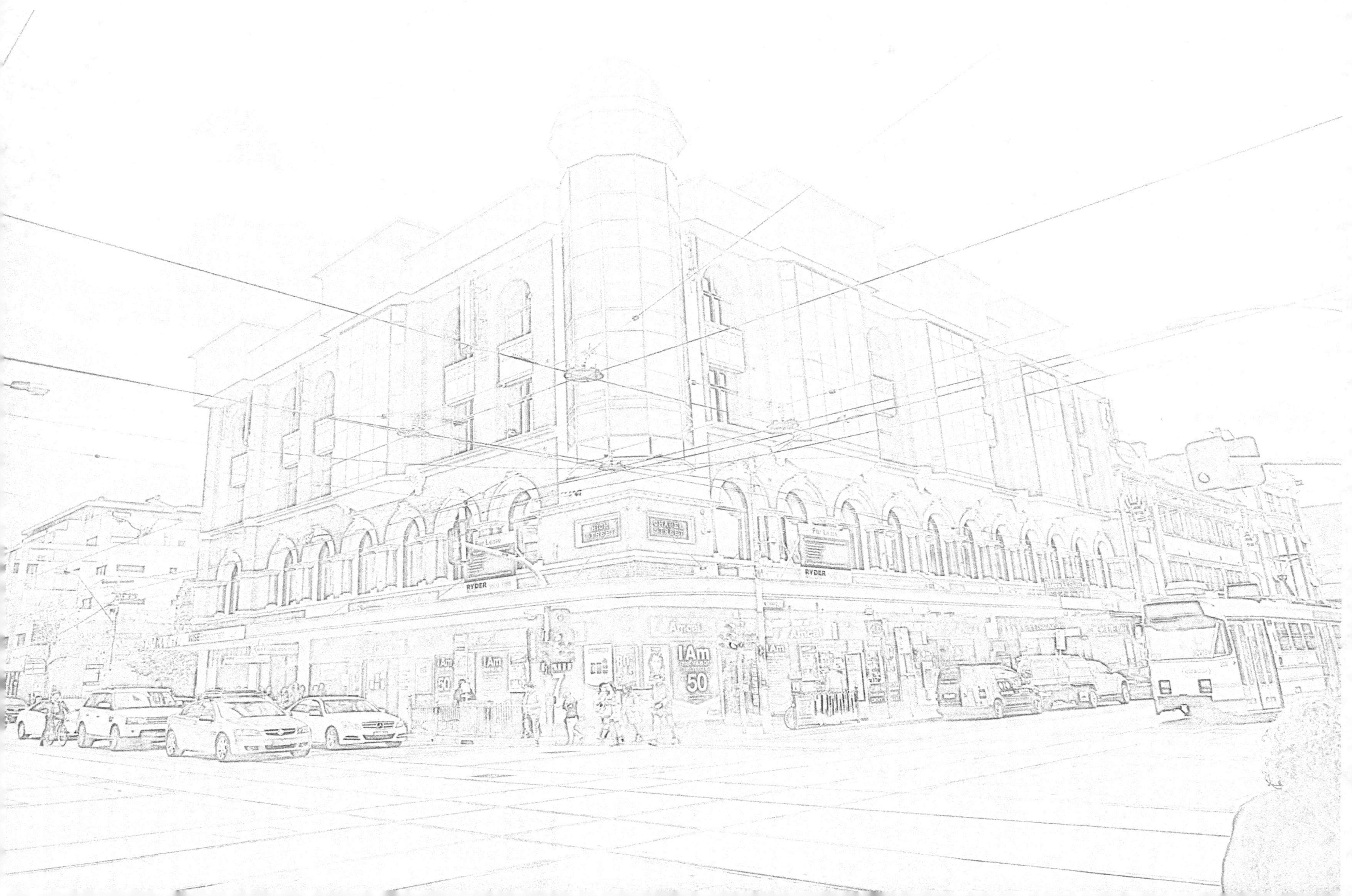

HIGH STREET
CHAPEL STREET
For Lease
RYDER
Amcal
IAm
50

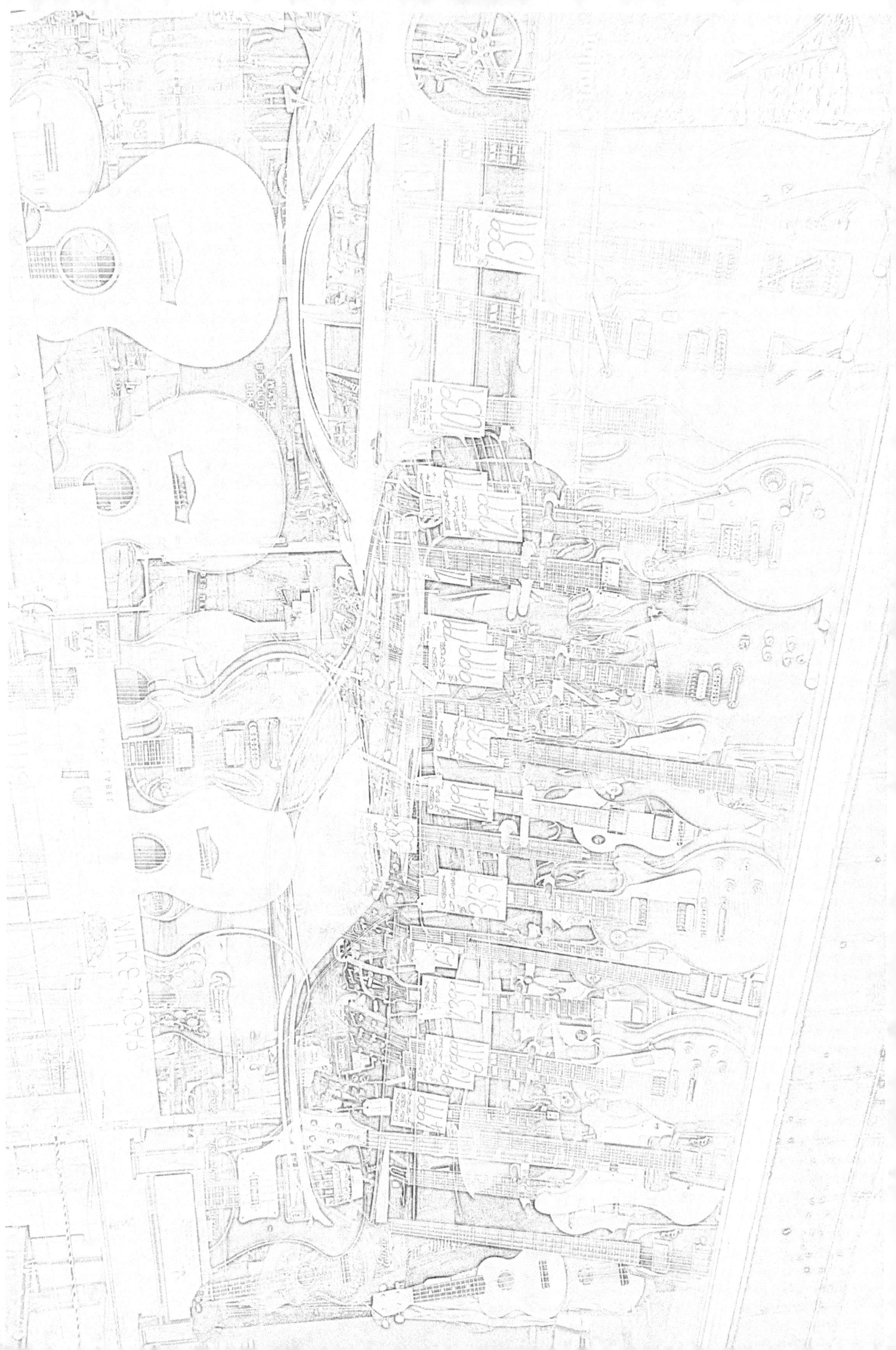

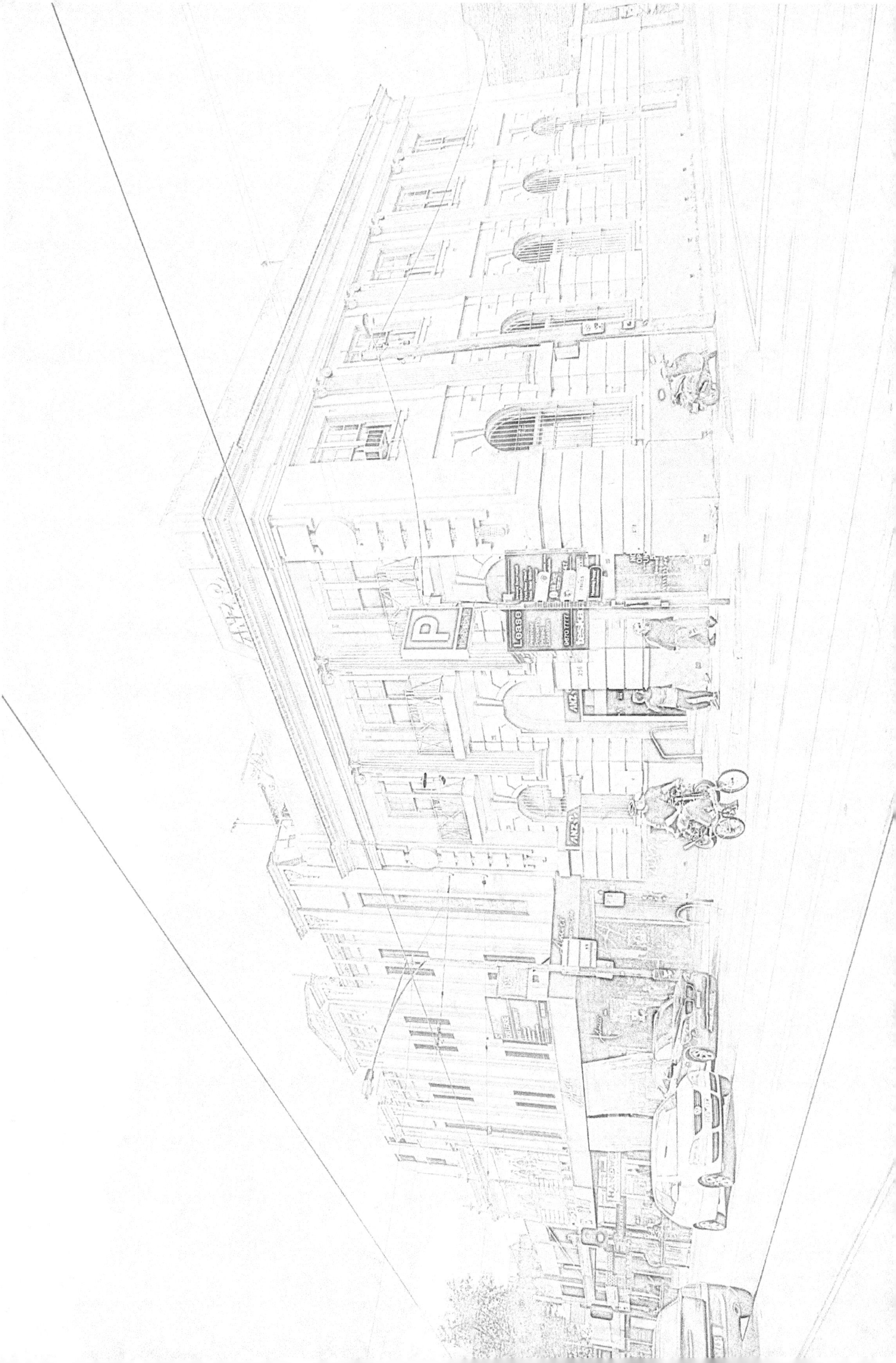
Lease
ANZ

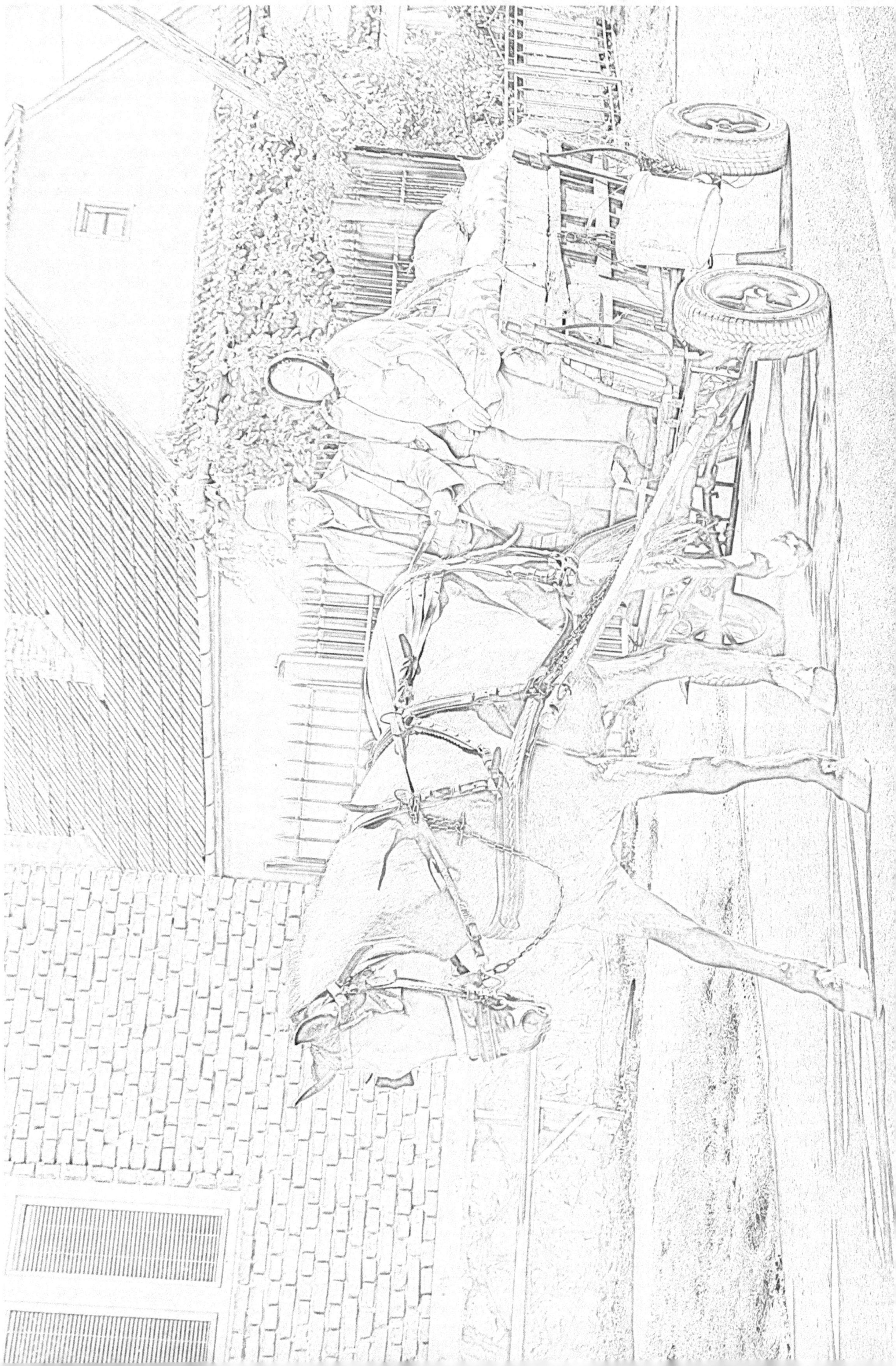

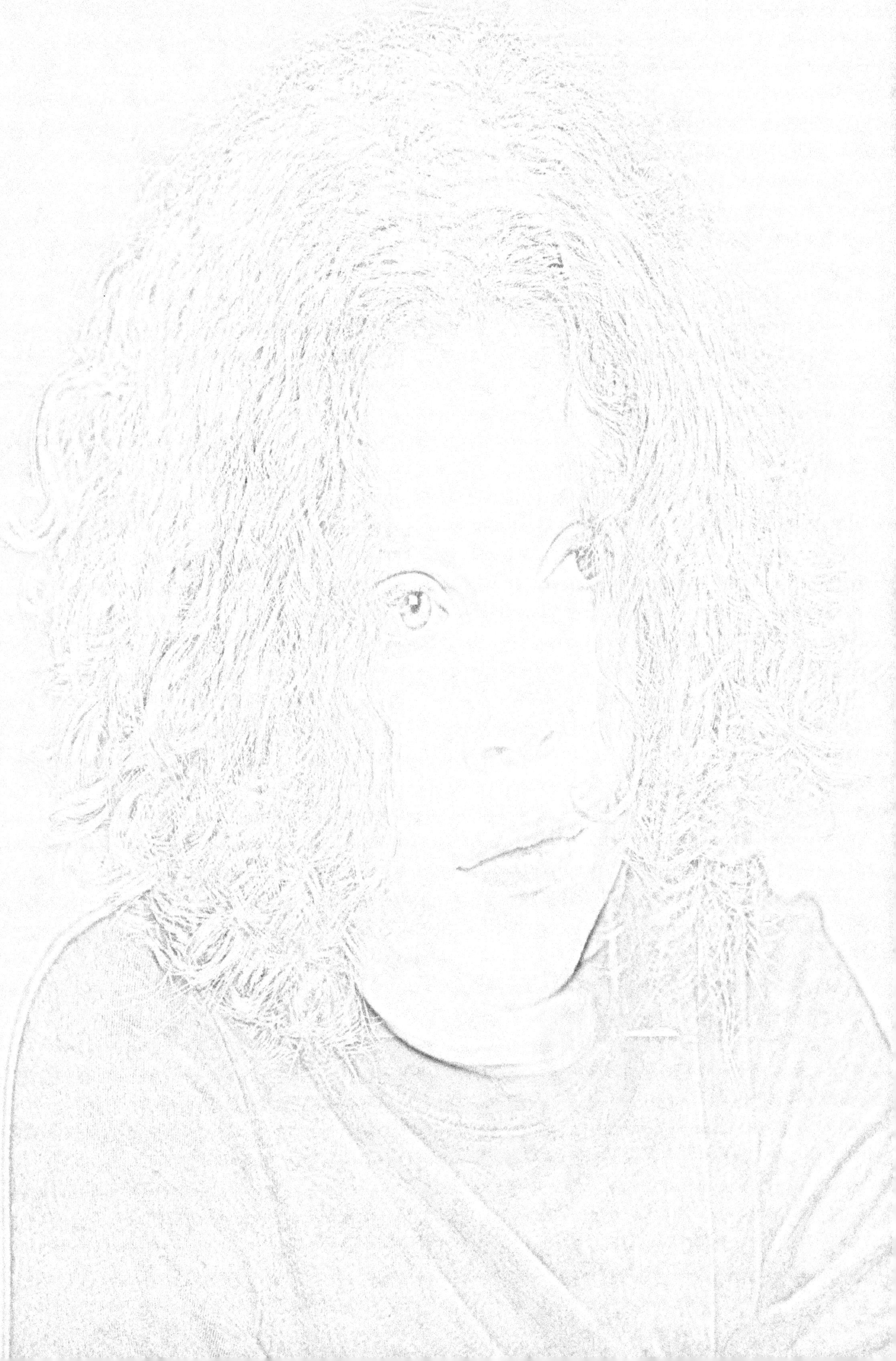

www.ingramcontent.com/pod-product-compliance
Lightning Source LLC
Chambersburg PA
CBHW081056180526
45170CB00005B/1782